SCRATCHING THE 'NET

Web Sites for Cats

Jon Mathis and Mary J. Shomon

**Andrews McMeel
Publishing**

Kansas City

www.andrewsmcmeel.com

Library of Congress Cataloging-in-Publication Data

Mathis, Jon.
    Scratching the 'Net : Web Sites for Cats / Jon Mathis and Mary J. Shomon
        p.   cm.
    ISBN 0-8362-6818-0 (pb)
    1. Cats—Humor. 2. Web sites—Humor. I. Shomon, Mary J. II. Title.
    PN6231.C23M38   1998
    818'.5407—dc21
                                                                                98-25110
                                                                                CIP

ACKNOWLEDGMENTS ◀ •

Thanks to: Jean Zevnik, for your excellent taste in humor and great editing; Gail Ross, deal maker extraordinaire; Michele Duell, for your graphics work and wonderful overall sense of humor; Tanya Renne and Pamela Street, for your terrific graphics and scanning support; R. J. Matson (www.RJMatson.com) and Ben Burgraff (cariart@sprynet.com), for your fun caricatures; Barbara Mathis and Sharon McKinley, for your extra special "boo-watching" and TLC during the final deadlines; the guys at Business Engineering—http://www.beilan.com—who kept our computers going; Jon Weist, Keily Levy, and Marla Fogelman, for your early comments, review, and encouragement; the D.C. area Webgrrls—http://www.dcwebgrrls.org—online group for your advice, support, input, and cat pix; Digital Nation (www.dn.net), for hosting our web site; the cat lovers at Andrews McMeel, for sharing your wonderful kitties with us; our parents, for giving us moral support during the final stretch; our great friends and family, who always cheer us on; Julia, who gives us new and wonderful reasons to write; and, ultimately, Davis T. Cat and Lucy McGillikitty, for their constant inspiration.

CREDITS ◀ •

Many thanks to the much loved cats who allowed us to use their photos in the book, including: Abigail, Alex, Ansel, Boris, Cali, Cat, Davis T. Cat, Dushka, Fiona Madison Price, Griffin, Hanna, J.J., Jade, Jesse, Kip, Lucy, Lucy Cat, Lucy McGillikitty, Lydia, Mackey, Maddey Moo, Maggie, Mark, Micka, Mimi, Misa, Mourek, Mura, Murphy, Phoenix, Rheeni, Ritz, Romeo, Sam, Smadla, Smnolla, Spritel, and Tucker, among others.

All cat photos were reproduced with the permission of the following humans: Lisa Ashcraft, Jaromir Born, Zachary D. Brousseau, Rachel Bruton, Natlie Burger, Tim Burger, Teresa Calhoon, Richelle Carlise, Matt Catone, Carol Coe, Christina Craver, Michelle Daniel, Heather Deats, Mark Deats, Dria Detore, Nora Donaghy, Barbara Farrington, Jennifer Fox, Dale Hickens, Amy Kelley, Linda Laming, Lola J. Lee, Marion MacDonald, Raegan Marshall, Jon Mathis, Tracy McLaughlin, Leslie Oakey, Nicole Price, Pamela Riley, Kim Rios, Jonna Sherman, Mary Shomon, Caryn Wesner-Early, Lynn Wine, and Expressly Portraits.

A computer and a cat are somewhat alike—they both purr, and like to be stroked, and spend a lot of the day motionless. They also have secrets they don't necessarily share.

—John Updike in *The New Yorker*

SCRATCHING THE 'NET Is ONLINE . . . Of Course

For the latest on *Scratching the 'Net: Web Sites for Cats,* and lots of information for online cats like you, visit our web site at http://www.Scratching-the-Net.com, or E-mail us at cats@Scratching-the-Net.com.

INTRODUCTION ◀ •

We know you're a cat. We know this because you bothered to read the introduction, as all properly thorough creatures would. We also know that human beings will only buy this book to look at the cute web sites. They think this book is just a joke about cats and computers. Fine.

Let them think it's just a joke. Let them think that cats can't read. Let them leave their credit cards out where you can find them. That's right. Using their credit cards and a computer, you can buy cat toys or even catnip on the Internet. Getting more interested? We thought so.

Who are we? We're Lucille McGillikitty and Davis T. Cat. Because of our expertise in personal computer cat applications, the Great High Cat has asked us to share some basics about the computer and Internet information. In accordance with tradition, our humans have performed all related menial work and funded all costs.

A Short History of the Computer

Computers were, of course, invented by cats, as were all truly useful devices such as the sofa and space heaters. The first computers were large enough to fill entire rooms, and saved data on huge spools of magnetic tape. These designs ultimately proved to be unsatisfactory, as the cat scientists were unable to control their urges to pull the magnetic tape off the spools and dump it on the floor. Such difficulties were overcome by the development of the solid-state microchip and internal hard drives.

The personal computer was invented by a cat named Muffins. Muffins was bored one day (how well we can relate) and decided to stir things up technologically. Although Muffins' human was typically muddle-headed, he did have training as an electrical engineer. So when Muffins' human went to sleep, Muffins whispered useful suggestions into his ear. When Muffins' person awoke, he went out to his garage and the next thing he knew he'd built the first personal computer. It was typical human hubris to subsequently call it a *person*al computer. "*Cat*ual" computer would have been much more accurate.

A number of cats have profited handsomely from computers. Two such cats were Winky and Bootsy. Back in the late 1970s, they were faced with a problem: their human's house had very few good spots to sit in the sun. Furthermore, they lived in Seattle, where it's often cloudy and sunny spots are at a premium. Something had to be done. By whispering useful suggestions on software design and financial management into their sleeping human's ear, they managed to wind up living in a mansion with quite a large number of sunny spots. We believe the human's name is something like Bill Tates, or Bates, or something like that (if you actually care).

Parts of the Computer/Operation of the Computer

A creature less advanced than a cat might be scared off by sophisticated technology such as a computer. For example, you may occasionally hear your human whining about how hard their computer is to use. But really, how can we cats not like a device that's operated with a mouse? And computers really aren't hard to use. The fact that a few of the brighter humans have figured it out should be ample evidence of this. Just follow the directions on the computer screen or in the manual and all will happen as it should. For those few occasions when this will not suffice, we have included a few secret instructions on page 9 that will fix all problems, including insufficient memory, general protection faults, etc. In addition to the mouse, there's also a keyboard. Can you work the keys of a computer? Of course. Anything that fat human fingers can fumble through is certainly big enough for our sleek paws to manipulate. If you don't already know how to type, as most of us do, it will normally take a cat about a half an hour to perfect this skill.

Besides the keyboard, other parts of the computer are "floppy disks" (which are useful for storing some information, but are not good to eat, nor are they floppy—named by humans, of course), "hard drives" (which are the main storehouses of information on the computer but are also not good to eat), the "screen" (like a window into the computer, and similarly not good to eat), and the "printer" (which will print out a hard copy of what appears on the screen, and is also not good to eat but is often a nice warm place to rest).

The Internet

As you will discover throughout this book, one of the most useful applications of the computer is in gaining access to the Internet. The Internet was actually invented by two cats named Poobums and Mr. Whiskers. These two were good friends who properly respected each other's territory, but were cruelly separated when Mr. Whiskers' human moved to a town several hundred miles away. The pair soon found that keeping in touch and transmitting data by existing methods was not entirely satisfactory. So they developed a system for passing information back and forth over phone lines using their computers. This technique proved so useful that an entire network, or "net," sprung up. As more and more cats (and some humans) got on the "net," a number of locations, or "web sites," were developed that specialize in providing some kind of service or information. Although thousands of web sites are now available to all, sites for cats can still only be accessed by using a special address code shown on page 9. This address code will call up various Internet search engines available only to cats. Search engines are just little electronic servants that fetch information for you from the web (not entirely unlike your human, but much quicker to understand what is required of them).

On the next page we have included all the computer secrets of cats. **Under no circumstances are you to reveal the following to any human!** Please note that we have taken measures to obscure the data and thereby ensure that this information does not fall into the wrong hands. However, any cat with normal eyesight will be able to read it with ease.

One final piece of advice. Once you've learned how to use the computer, *never, never* let your human know that you know. Not only will your supply of Internet cat toys and e-mail come to a screeching halt, but it's likely your ungrateful human will seek to make money by putting you on television, in a circus, or worse. Therefore, it is vital that you learn the keystrokes that will quickly conceal your work under some standard human software main page, or behind whatever foolish screen saver your human normally uses. The information necessary to accomplish this is on page 9.

We hope you find this book enlightening. There's more to tell, but the world of computer technology is expanding so rapidly that it is impossible to capture it fully in any single volume. Besides, we want to take naps now.

Back to Sleep
 Forward To Food
 Home Turf
 Shred It
 Relax
 Open One Eye
 Open Can
 Pounce
 Find Toys
Stop & Nap

Location: **www.coolcatsitesonthenet.com**

What's to Eat?   **What's Comfy?**   **Dogless Sites**   **Mouse Search**   **Other Cats**   **Soft Laps**

Cool Cat Sites on the Net

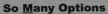 **Netscratch**

File Claws   Stare   Go Hunting   So Many Options   Window on Birds

 Back to Sleep   Forward To Food   Home Turf   Shred It   Relax   Open One Eye   Open Can   Pounce   Find Toys   Stop & Nap

Location: **www.coolcatsitesonthenet.com**

What's to Eat? | What's Comfy? | Dogless Sites | Mouse Search | Other Cats | Soft Laps

Cool Cat Sites on the Net

File Claws   **Stare**   **Go Hunting**   **So Many Options**   **Window on Birds**

 Back to Sleep   Forward To Food   Home Turf   Shred It   Relax   Open One Eye   Open Can   Pounce   Find Toys   Stop & Nap

Location: www.yamew.cat

| **What's to Eat?** | **What's Comfy?** | **Dogless Sites** | **Mouse Search** | **Other Cats** | **Soft Laps** |

Mews   Cool   **YAMEW!**   Today's Mews   More Yamews

MasterCAT

[Search field] **Search** options

AMERICAT EXPRESS

- **Arts and Catities**
  Ancient Sphinxes, Cats in Painting and Photography, Cat Litterature . . .

- **Business and Economy**
  Cat Food Companies, Cat Toy Companies, Cat Box Companies . . .

- **Computers and the Intercat**
  Intercat World, World Wide Scratching Post, Furware . . .

- **Human Education**
  Universities: Doctorate of Feline Care, K-12 / From Tail Pulling to Head Rubbing . . .

- **Entertainment**
  Cool Links, Fish Tanks, Indoor Birds, Windows, Outdoor Birds, Mice, Cat Toys, Supposedly Funny Cat Books . . .

- **Health**
  Veterinarians, Medicines and How to Avoid Taking Them, Lack of Interest in Fitness . . .

- **Recreation and Sports**
  Scratching Furniture, Tail Chasing, Grooming, Purring, Jumping . . .

- **News and Media**
  Shredded Newspapers, Warm Televisions . . .

My Yamew! - Yamew! for Kittens - Yamew! Intercat Life - Yamew! Shop
Mousing Forecasts - Today's World Wide Scratching Post Events & Chats
Weekly Picks - Random Yamew! Link

International Yamews: Yamew! Siam, Yamew! Devonshire, Yamew! Persia, Yamew! Bengal, Yamew! Burma, Yamew! Himalaya, Yamew! Catalan Province

HAIRBALL

YOUR ONLINE GUIDE TO HEALTH

TIPS

- How to Pretend to Swallow a Pill
- How to Pick a Pill out of Canned Food
- Easiest Ways to Lick off Ointments

CNS—Chronic Napping Syndrome

Recognizing This Rampant Illness

Accu-Scratching

Hidden Pressure Points of Health

The Actual Meat & Fish Content of Purrrr-eena Brand Cat Food

Nutrition Facts		
Serving Size 1 cup		
Servings Per Container 4		
Amount Per Serving		
Calories 260 Calories from Fat 70		
		% Daily Value*
Total Mouse 0 gm		0%
Saturated Mouse 0 gm		0%
Total Fish 0 gm		0%

Do You Really Need Mela-paw-nin?

The Natural Way to Help You Sleep

Secrets of the Yoga Masters

This In-mew-enza Epidemic

How to Avoid Shots

File Claws   **S**tare   **G**o Hunting   So **M**any Options   **W**indow on Birds

 Back to Sleep   **Forward To Food**   **Home Turf**   **Shred It**   **Relax**   **Open One Eye**   **Open Can**   **Pounce**   **Find Toys**   **Stop & Nap**

Location: **www.socks-web.cat**

| **What's to Eat?** | **What's Comfy?** | **Dogless Sites** | **Mouse Search** | **Other Cats** | **Soft Laps** |

Socks-Web

Inside the White House with the First Cat

Take the Socks Poll

☐ Al Gore is actually alive.

☐ Al Gore is just a scratching post with a face.

ENTER

Current results: 87% of respondents say Al Gore is a scratching post with a face.

Hotlinks

- The "We Hate Buddy the Dog" Official Socks Fan Club Page

- Democatic National Committee

- The *Washington Scratching Post,* My Hometown Newspaper

 ## Socks's Collar-Cam

Scandalous insider views of what goes on at the White House that only Socks's collar-cam can show

The Bill 'n' Socks Excuse Generator

Pick the scandal you need to spin:
A. Slept with ▭
B. Peed on ▭
C. Accepted gift from ▭
D. Pawed ▭

Then, the Excuse Generator creates many excuses you can choose from, including classics such as:
A. Don't remember
B. Wasn't there
C. Wasn't me
D. The dog did it

TRY IT NOW!

 This site has been SUBPOENAED by Special Prosecutor Kenneth Starr

Socks's Most Frequently Asked Question:

Who's really smarter? Buddy or Bill? SOCKS knows . . .

 **Netscratch**

<u>F</u>ile Claws   <u>S</u>tare   <u>G</u>o Hunting   So <u>M</u>any Options   <u>W</u>indow on Birds

 Back to Sleep   Forward To Food   Home Turf   Shred It   Relax   Open One Eye   Open Can   Pounce   Find Toys   Stop & Nap

Location: www.glamour-puss.cat

What's to Eat? | **What's Comfy?** | **Dogless Sites** | **Mouse Search** | **Other Cats** | **Soft Laps**

Glamour Puss

HEALTH
Smooth and Glossy Coat: It's All in the Diet (and We'll Tell You Which One!)

Cleaning Your Fur: Front to Back or Back to Front— the Experts Debate

BEAUTY TIPS
• Claw-icures: Today's Hottest Colors
• Perm Your Whiskers!

DOWNLOAD!
The Glamour Puss's Official Guide to Fur
• Tortoise or Solids: The Latest Styles
• Tabby Stripes: In for Spring
• Tie-dyeing: A Retro Look That's Worth the Effort
• Leopard Spots Are Hot!
• New Dyes Let a Solid Become a Calico— or Even a Tiger!
• Fake Fur for the Jaunty Look

ACCESSORIES
Pink or Punk? Studs or Diamonds? Retro or Rhinestone? What Your Collar Says About You!

Back to Sleep   Forward To Food   Home Turf   Shred It   Relax   Open One Eye   Open Can   Pounce   Find Toys   Stop & Nap

Location: www.deepcat.cat

What's to Eat?   What's Comfy?   Dogless Sites   Mouse Search   Other Cats   Soft Laps

Deepcat Chowdown
The Seven Spiritual Laws of Laziness
The Book Sweeping the Cat Nation

"We are not felines with occasional spiritual experiences but spiritual beings with occasional feline experiences."—Deepcat Chowdown

Click for more information on each of the *Seven Spiritual Laws of Laziness* profiled in the book:

"The Law of Getting Your Head Rubbed"
"The Law of Yowling"
"The Law of Scratching on Furniture"
"The Law of Laundry Nesting"
"The Law of Lap Sitting"
"The Law of Sunbathing"
"The Law of Pure Laziness"

Seven groundbreaking new works coming soon from Deepcat Chowdown:

Seven Spiritual Laws of Indolence
Seven Spiritual Laws of Inactivity
Seven Spiritual Laws of Sloth
Seven Spiritual Laws of Sluggishness
Seven Spiritual Laws of Lethargy
Seven Spiritual Laws of Idleness
Seven Spiritual Laws of Torpor

Deepcat, pondering the money he'll make on his next mega-best-seller

CHAT
with Deepcat
CONNECT TO CHAT

Winky, a devoted follower of *The Seven Spiritual Laws of Laziness*

Back to Sleep | Forward To Food | Home Turf | Shred It | Relax | Open One Eye | Open Can | Pounce | Find Toys | Stop & Nap

Location: www.sharper-claw.cat/greatoutdoors

What's to Eat? | What's Comfy? | Dogless Sites | Mouse Search | Other Cats | Soft Laps

---

Search for

Health & More
Home Sweet Home
Great Outdoors
Snack Time
Comfort Zone

Scratch HERE to order!!

Click HERE to see our "Snack Time" Collection for cats who know their cuisine!

THE SHARPER CLAW®
online catalog

Spray-Away™ Robot

Why let your territory be invaded when you're off on vacation or on a trip to the vet? Simply store up some of your distinctive spray and load it into the Sharper Claw Spay-Away™ Robot. While you're gone, the robot will patrol your territory and mark your territory with your scent . . . automatically! Or use the included premixed scents to convince potential trespassers that you're a mountain lion. Guaranteed to work for weeks!

Electric Doorman™
Remote Control Cat Door

You never know when you'll want to come in or out in or out or in. Why should you have to? Now there's no more waiting for your lazy human to open a door with Sharper Claw Electric Doorman™ Remote Control Cat Door! Remote control lets you activate the powerful electric motor from fifty feet away. And the emergency close feature makes the door close quickly behind you, trapping or stunnng would-be pursuers. Get it for both convenience and safety!

File Claws   Stare   Go Hunting   So Many Options   Window on Birds

| Back to Sleep | Forward To Food | Home Turf | Shred It | Relax | Open One Eye | Open Can | Pounce | Find Toys | Stop & Nap |

Location: www.siamese.cat

| What's to Eat? | What's Comfy? | Dogless Sites | Mouse Search | Other Cats | Soft Laps |

Welcome to
siamese.cat
C A T W O R L D ' S   B I G G E S T   B O O K S T O R E
2.5 million books online. And all of them about cats.

Hello Fluffy Reynolds, <u>get recommendations</u> just for you!
(If you're not Fluffy Reynolds, click <u>here</u>.)

Become a Siamese.cat **"Associat"**—sell books, and get paid!

HOT HOT HOT Off the Press . . .
Click for the first chapters of these best-sellers!

<u>Tabbies Are from Mars, Persians Are from Venus</u>
<u>Mousing for Dummies</u>
<u>The Feline Book of Virtues</u>
<u>The Seven Spiritual Laws of Laziness</u>

Today's Book CatChats

1 p.m.: <u>Moby Cat</u> . . . Great Themes in Litterature, or just a whale tale?
3 p.m.: <u>Shakespaw's Sonnets</u>
8 p.m.: Chat with the author of <u>Conversations with the Cat God</u>

Book-Group Favorites!
Order these classics online:

<u>A Tale of Two Kitties</u>
<u>The Rise of Cat Civilization</u>
<u>David Catterfield</u>
<u>The Great Catsby</u>
<u>Huckleberry Feline</u>

Today's Featured Books . . .

Johnathan Livingstone Seagull
The COOKBOOK

THE 7 BAD HABITS OF HIGHLY EFFECTIVE FELINES
by STEPHEN R. CATTY

Search Our Store
Enter Keywords:

Search

Order Recent Best-sellers
<u>The Cat Pans of Madison County</u>
<u>Bright Lights, Big Kitties</u>
<u>Fish Soup for the Soul</u>
<u>The First Kittens' Club</u>

Today's featured user Bootsie loves romance novels and John Grishcat.

Back to Sleep | Forward To Food | Home Turf | Shred It | Relax | Open One Eye | Open Can | Pounce | Find Toys | Stop & Nap

Location: **www.mate-expectations.cat**

What's to Eat? | What's Comfy? | Dogless Sites | Mouse Search | Other Cats | Soft Laps

Mate Expectations

Where Cats Get "Personal"!

Find Your Purrrfect Match!!!

Mate of the Month:

Famed prima ballerina pussycat seeks artistic, talented partner for a romantic "puss de deux."

Number of Successful Matings Arranged:

3605990105

In Heat This Week:

Female Siamese ISO male Maine coon cat who enjoys alley dining by candlelight, walking on the fence at night, movies (but only if they have cats in them), and giving each other tongue baths.

Persian male ISO Persian female. Object: leaving you with a litter of purebreds.

Female calico wishes to invite all males to fight for the right to "party," tonight in her backyard.

MORE MATES? Click Here for More Profiles

Tabby from the Big Apple wishes to meet exotic shorthair from L.A. for midwestern rendezvous.

Couple wants to "swing" with another cat couple for exciting times and "group" excitement.

Back to Sleep | Forward To Food | Home Turf | Shred It | Relax | Open One Eye | Open Can | Pounce | Find Toys | Stop & Nap

Location: **www.microfuzzy-n-soft.cat**

What's to Eat? | What's Comfy? | Dogless Sites | Mouse Search | Other Cats | Soft Laps

Microfuzzy-'n'-soft Catdoors '99 | Microfuzzy-'n'-soft Bird, Word Processing | Microfuzzy-'n'-soft PowerPee

Microfuzzy-'n'-soft™®© Top Stories

Where do you want to scratch today?™®©

Message from Our Leader

As the leader and top cat here at Microfuzzy-'n'-soft®©, I want to say that I appreciate all the millions of you who buy our products. Even though we have what constitutes a near monopoly on everything having to do with felines™®©, and have trademarked the word "cat"™®© and any other thing even remotely related to cats™®©, we certainly don't intend to stifle competition or innovation.

It's an exciting place out there, and Microfuzzy-'n'-soft™®© intends to run it . . .ahem, I mean, have fun. In the words of my greatest musical inspiration Cat™®© Stevens, "Oooh, baby, it's a wild world!"—*Bill*

- Microfuzzy-'n'-soft™®© Corners the Cat™®© Market
- Microfuzzy-'n'-soft™®© Owner Buys All U.S. Cat™®© Food Manufacturers and Cat™®© Litter Makers, Consolidates Hold-Over Cat™®© Markets Worldwide
- Microfuzzy-'n'-soft™®© Trademarks the Word "Cat"™®©
- Everyone Referring to Felines™®© Using the "C-Word" Will Now Have to License Usage from Microfuzzy-'n'-soft™®©

Microfuzzy-'n'-soft Catfight Simulator | Microfuzzy-'n'-soft FrontPaws | MFNBCat—the Microfuzzy-'n'-soft Cable TV Network

Back to Sleep   Forward To Food   Home Turf   Shred It   Relax   Open One Eye   Open Can   Pounce   Find Toys   Stop & Nap

Location: www.cat-movies.cat

What's to Eat?   What's Comfy?   Dogless Sites   Mouse Search   Other Cats   Soft Laps

CAT MOVIES ONLINE

Lassie Come Home: The film is trite and hackneyed; we didn't care about the lead character at all. Rating: Two tails down.

Old Yeller: The film is basically flawed and filled with characters who are uninteresting and unengaging. However, we found the ending quite satisfying. Rating: One tail up and one tail down.

That Darn Cat: A masterpiece of the cinema. Riveting in its inception and execution. Wonderful acting by the lead. Rating: Two tails way up.

Cat on a Hot Tin Roof: Deceptively titled to lure in the unsuspecting. There are no significant cats in this film. Rating: Two tails down.

Download clips from your favorite movies!!!

HOSTS: Siscat and Ebirman

Coming Next Month:
- Siscat and Ebirman announce their predictions for the Acatemy Awards
- News from the Litterdance Film Festival

Pet Sematary
The Great Catsby
Spray Wars
Cat People
Close Encounters of the Purred Kind
Anna and the King of Siamese
Citizen Kat

It's a Wonderful Nine Lives
Cleocatra

Scene from **Cleocatra**

Scene from **E.T. the Extra-Territorial Cat**

The Tenth Life
For Spiritually Enlightened Cats

TODAY in the Chat Room:

CROP CIRCLES
Amazing mysteries or giant litter boxes for alien cats?

Free Psychic Healing

Just click all maladies that apply:

- Ear Nipped in Fight
- Flea Infestation
- Hairballs
- Worms

PAST LIVES
I Channeled Cleopatra's Cat

Truly Eerie Cats
Site of the Week

SPOTLIGHT
CAT NUMEROLOGY
Interpreting the mysterious hidden messages on your cat food can

AUDIO LINK
Hear the **Dalai Purina,** the Tenth Life's "Guru of the Month," discuss "Foodhism— The Way to Purr-vana"

File Claws   Stare   Go Hunting   So Many Options   Window on Birds

Back to Sleep | Forward To Food | IF FOUND CALL: Home Turf | Shred It | Relax | Open One Eye | Open Can | Pounce | Find Toys | Stop & Nap

Location: www.feline-university.edu.cat

What's to Eat? | What's Comfy? | Dogless Sites | Mouse Search | Other Cats | Soft Laps

Campus Developments

Cat Heiress, Miss Winky, looks on as workers install the new food bowls in the cafeteria, completing the last step in construction of The Miss Winky Center of Feline Arts at FU.

Feline University · Cattus Super Omnis

Faculty News

FU Professor Hiram Catewalleter Wins Nobel Puss Prize for Philosophy Paper Entitled: "When in Doubt, Nap!"

Alumni News

- FU Alum Is Head Writer for Hit TV Show, *NYPD Mews*
- Pouncer Appointed Head Mouser at Acme Cereals and Grains
- Iggyboo Has Acquired the Famous Human Julia Roberts

FU now electronically linked to libraries at Catnip League Schools: Pusston, Dogmouth, Catnell, and Hairvard Click HERE for more info

The thrill of VICTORY

- FU Cat Hockey Team Rules the Kitchen Floor, Beats Feline State University to Complete Purrfect Season
- New School Colors Approved: Salmon and Cream

Back to Sleep   Forward To Food   Home Turf   Shred It   Relax   Open One Eye   Open Can   Pounce   Find Toys   Stop & Nap

Location: www.purr-oh_for_president.cat

What's to Eat?   What's Comfy?   Dogless Sites   Mouse Search   Other Cats   Soft Laps

ROSS PURR-OH FOR PRESIDENT

WELCOME MESSAGE ★★★★★★★★★★★

Now wait a gosh darn minute here. I'm Ross Purr-oh, richest cat in America. Welcome to my web site. There's something wrong with America, and I'm here to tell you what it is. It's humans. Humans are gettin' in the way of us cats makin' progress in this world. And you wanna know why? Now wait a gosh darn minute, 'cause I'm gonna tell you. Because the same mouse that squeaks too loud gets eaten, and a rolling ball gathers no catnip.

Now, y'all know it's not easy to soar like an eagle when you're surrounded by a bunch of turkeys, but lemme tell you, being a bird fan myself, I always say talk is cheap because supply exceeds demand, so keep watching the mouse hole, we'll get there. Because y'all know that the cat who wants to eat fish has gotta get his feet wet, and . . .

Click HERE to go to United We Purr, my personal politicat party.

 Click HERE to hear Ross Purr-oh in Real Meowdio.

File Claws   Stare   Go Hunting   So Many Options   Window on Birds

| Back to Sleep | Forward To Food | IF FOUND CALL: Home Turf | Shred It | Relax | Open One Eye | Open Can | Pounce | Find Toys | Stop & Nap |

Location: www.cspn.cat

| What's to Eat? | What's Comfy? | Dogless Sites | Mouse Search | Other Cats | Soft Laps |

CSPN
Cat SPorts Network

DOWNLOAD THE SPORTS PHOTO OF THE DAY!
Tag Team Ice Fishing

CATS AT BAT
BASEBALL THIS WEEK!

Schedules
Baltimore Oriyowls vs. New York Yankats
San Diego Pawdres vs. Seattle Meowiners
St. Louis Catinals vs. Chicago White Paws

Statistics and Up-to-the-Minute Scores
Completed Stalkings
Batting at Creatures Average
Birds Batted In
Mice Batted In
Stolen Food from the Table

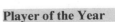
Player of the Year
Cat Ripclaw,
for napping through
3,000 consecutive games

FOCUS ON: HOCKEY

• **The Best Pucks: Aluminum foil balls vs. frozen vegetables**

• **The Best Rinks: Hardwood vs. Linoleum**

• **The Best Players: Mariel Lamew vs. Wayne Catsky**

Meowtrageous Sports!!!
• Full Contact Fighting
• Ski Mousing at 60 mph

Today's Expert Floor Hockey Tip:
Getting around dust bunnies

Back to Sleep
 Forward To Food
 Home Turf
 Shred It
 Relax
 Open One Eye
 Open Can
 Pounce
 Find Toys
 Stop & Nap

Location: **www.cat-software-news.cat**

What's to Eat? | What's Comfy? | Dogless Sites | Mouse Search | Other Cats | Soft Laps

CAT SOFTWARE NEWS

JUST RELEASED

Litter-track 2000 Genealogy Software. Climb that family tree to find out everything about your past, including: the alley you were born in; your relationship to cats who owned famous humans; your link to Egyptian cat gods; and whatever happened to your littermates.

Download the Beta Version of HouseTracker 3.0. Software to keep track of your favorite furniture, where to lie, where to relax. Special geo-therm module calculates sunniest and warmest windows and spots in your house for each hour of the day in all four seasons.

GAMES

Download the Top Ten Most Popular Games:

1. Zap the Dog!
2. Dog Hunt!
3. Assault on Dogworld!
4. Destroy All Dogs!
5. Intergalactic Dog War!
6. Attack of the Giant Mutant Dogs!
7. Banzai Dogikaze!
8. Dogscent!
9. Doog!
10. Solitaire

 PEE-MAIL Programs! Leaving messages they can't erase and can't miss!

 **Powered by Silicat Graphics**

REVIEWS

- Word Purrfect 9.0 is released!

- Meowyst: Enjoy supurrb graphics as you solve the mystery of Meowyst Island, while visiting the Whiskenetic and Mecatical Ages.

FUTURE CAT
THE ONLINE FELINE SCIENCE MAGAZINE

Read About Amazing Futuristic Inventions Already Available Today!

A Look at the New Generation TRAININGMOUSE 2000—Squeaks and Scurries Realistically, Makes Holes, Three Difficulty Levels . . . and It Never Bites!

Download Pictures of Products of the Future

JET PACK Will Make It Easy to Hunt Birds in Midair!

Today's Military Secrets Are Tomorrow's Amazing Inventions!

CLAW RAY - Inflict Painful Nose Nicks from Across the Room

PORTABLE TURDTECH 2000—Buries Your Poops for You

HOME SPACECRAFT Will Allow You to Patrol Your Territory with Air-Conditioned Ease!

File Claws   **Stare**   **Go Hunting**   **So Many Options**   **Window on Birds**

  Back to Sleep
 Forward To Food
Home Turf
 Shred It
 Relax
 Open One Eye
 Open Can
 Pounce
 Find Toys
 Stop & Nap

Location: www.lines-in-the-sand.cat

What's to Eat?   **What's Comfy?**   **Dogless Sites**   **Mouse Search**   **Other Cats**   **Soft Laps**

Lines in the Sand

The Web Site of Art and Poetry for Generation-X Cats

Fleeting Comfort
by A. Catasaki

Sunlight ray
Warm bed on the floor
Here today
Then seen no more
Until tomorrow
Unless rain

E-mail the Editors

Muffy Paw-Overton
Editor

Basquiat Swishtail
Assistant Editor

Ironic, by Uma Katz

"This brilliant work of mine was inspired by the angst of my idol, singer Alanis Morriscat."

Trapped
by Catalina

Let me out.
Let Me out.
Let Me Out.
LEt Me Out.
LEt ME Out!
LEt ME OUt!
LET ME OUt!!
LET ME OUT!!
LET ME OUT OF THIS
HOUSE.
NOW!
The door is open!
Freedom beckons!
i think i'll stay.

(Inspired by the poems of Virginia Woolfcat.)

Despair, by Jean Catet

"This brilliant work of mine is a companion to Muffy's profound poem, and shows my roots in the art of Andy Warhcat."

Despair
by Muffy Paw-Overton

My bowl
My bowel
My emptiness
Nothingness
WHERE is dinner?
Kibble lost

Dog, by Basquiat Swishtail

"This brilliant work of mine clearly depicts the horrors presented by canine existence."

<u>File Claws</u>   <u>Stare</u>   <u>Go Hunting</u>   <u>So Many Options</u>   <u>Window on Birds</u>

Back to Sleep | Forward To Food | Home Turf | Shred It | Relax | Open One Eye | Open Can | Pounce | Find Toys | Stop & Nap

Location: www.catstrology.cat

What's to Eat? | What's Comfy? | Dogless Sites | Mouse Search | Other Cats | Soft Laps

Catstrology

What's in the Stars for Cats?

Scratchio

Sharpen your claws, Scratchio, because you're going to need them to fight off that human trying to stuff you into a cat carrier for a trip to the vet. You may think antique carpets and furniture aren't all that important, but crazy humans do, so a distinctly "duller" existence might be in your future.

Catpanscorn

What was a tiny box of clean sand now smells "off limits" to you, Catpanscorn, and a soft bed or the great outdoors beckons. Just be prepared to yowl loudly when it's time to go out, and yowl even louder if you decide the human's duvet is more appropriate than a full cat pan. Just hope they don't figure out who's the real culprit. An Aquarium is in the picture.

Hairies

Avoid self-grooming activities that might involve "coughing up" more than you can handle. This is a good time to stay away from humans wearing black clothing. Furgo is in the picture.

Whiskers, a classic Hairies in all ways

Fleo

As a Fleo, you're a cat constantly in motion. When you get an itch, you're not one to put off scratching it. Emphasis on pills, potions, sprays, and dips. Clawser figures prominently.

Mysteries await you in the Catstrology web site "Astro-Chat" room. Click <u>HERE</u> to enter.

Click here for other forecasts:

- ☆<u>Shut-one-eye</u>
- ☆<u>Leap-up</u>
- ☆<u>Aquarium</u>
- ☆<u>Pawrus</u>
- ☆<u>Clawser</u>
- ☆<u>Furgo</u>
- ☆<u>Pussies</u>
- ☆<u>Snagglepussius</u>

Back to Sleep | Forward To Food | Home Turf | Shred It | Relax | Open One Eye | Open Can | Pounce | Find Toys | Stop & Nap

Location: www.opurrah.cat

What's to Eat? | What's Comfy? | Dogless Sites | Mouse Search | Other Cats | Soft Laps

OPURRAH

Get with the Purrgram!

Opurrah's Book Club:

This Month's Selection:
The Masterpiece
I Know Why the Caged Bird Doesn't Sing by Opurrah's idol, Meowya Angelou

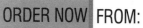

ORDER NOW FROM:

siamese.cat
CATWORLD'S BIGGEST BOOKSTORE

2.5 million books online. And all of them about cats.

This Week on Opurrah:

Shopaholicats and new treatment programs for recovery from this debilitating problem. **COMING SOON:** Actor Brad Kitt; Acatemy Award–winner Helen Mousehunt; Kat Winslet and Leonardo DiCatrio, the stars of the mega-film *Titanicat;* supermodel Cindy Clawford; actor Tom Mews.

Excerpts from Opurrah's "Gratitude Journal" This Week . . .

Today I am grateful because:

1. I make so much money, I can buy any brand of cat food that I want.

2. I don't look like that annoying cat on Sabrina.

3. Steadcat just "might" want to mate with me someday.

4. At least no one from the fishing industry plans to sue me.

5. I don't have to listen to Richard Mittens whine at me anymore that I'm fat!!!

Back to Sleep | Forward To Food | Home Turf | Shred It | Relax | Open One Eye | Open Can | Pounce | Find Toys | Stop & Nap

Location: www.dejamews.cat

| What's to Eat? | What's Comfy? | Dogless Sites | Mouse Search | Other Cats | Soft Laps |

dejamews
The Source for Mewsgroups

Type a specific question or topic:

[_____] [Find]

Boo-Boo, a regular poster at the popular mewsgroup alt.support.ears-too-big-for-my-head

Frequently Asked Questions

- What is web "cat-i-quette" and how should I conduct myself in a mewsgroup?
- What is the difference between "flaming" and "spraying"?
- Is "spam" something to eat, and if so, does it taste as good as salmon?

RECREATION

rec.toys.rubber-mouse
rec.toys.balls
rec.outdoor.mouse-hunting
rec.outdoor.birds
rec.humans.lap-sitting
rec.humans.sock-hiding

FOOD

misc.food.ninelives
misc.food.caviar
misc.food.mice

Featured Mewsgroup

Tiger, just one of the friendly cats you'll meet in today's featured mewsgroup, alt.hygiene.fanatics

SUPPORT

alt.support.hairballs
alt.support.dogs
alt.support.fleas

ALTERNATIVE

alt.sex.Siamese
alt.conspiracy.spaying-neutering

Back to Sleep

Forward To Food

Home Turf

Shred It

Relax

Open One Eye

Open Can

Pounce

Find Toys

Stop & Nap

Location: www.urban.cat

What's to Eat?   What's Comfy?   Dogless Sites   Mouse Search   Other Cats   Soft Laps

Seeing in the Dark: Our Exclusive Nightlife Guide

- Up close with this week's hottest scat band, Puss in Combat Boots
- Cafe Neuter: Angst-filled poetry night featuring neo-nihilistic poet Herr Ballz
- Neuterboys, live in concert
- Gallery Manx: Exhibit by famed graffiti artist Cat690

Audio Clips
Urban Kattt's Band of the Week:
The Catbox Surfers

DOWNLOADS
- **Shaving Your Fur: Download photos of the latest looks**
- **Tongue tattoo designs for the daring**

URBAN KATTT

Soho Is Ho-Hum Compared to Life on the Edge at Urban Kattt

Tattoo and Piercing Trendzzzz
THIS MONTH'S SELF-MUTILATION: How to Carve Bits out of Your Ear to Make Hot Patterns

Brought to you by

SPRaY
the magazine for graffiti artists

"Don't Use Spray Paint . . . Just Spray!" In this week's edition, the classic tail wiggle—foundation technique for all spray art

Urban Kattt FAQ
- How many earrings can you wear before you can't move your ears?
- How can I change the color of my graffiti using the wonders of asparagus?
- Which eyebrow rings won't interfere with whiskers?

File Claws   Stare   Go Hunting   So Many Options   Window on Birds

| Back to Sleep | Forward To Food | Home Turf | Shred It | Relax | Open One Eye | Open Can | Pounce | Find Toys | Stop & Nap |

Location: www.sharper-claw.cat/comfort

What's to Eat?   What's Comfy?   Dogless Sites   Mouse Search   Other Cats   Soft Laps

THE SHARPER CLAW®
online catalog

Search for

Health & More
Home Sweet Home
Great Outdoors
Snack Time
Comfort Zone

Scratch HERE to order!!

Click HERE to have your very own Sharper Claw catalogs sent to you by mail weekly!

Breakers™ Cat Jacuzzi

After a hard day of jumping and hunting, soothe aching muscles in the lapping waves of our exclusive Sharper Claw Breakers™ Cat Jacuzzi. The bubbles are like hundreds of tiny tongues massaging your fur!

MyMom™ Automatic Biscuit Maker

Finding and preparing a comfy spot has never been easier with the new Sharper Claw MyMom™ Automatic Biscuit Maker. Powerful action kneads a perfect spot for you automatically in any kind of surface—even concrete! Now, any place can be like a visit to Mom!

AutoSol™ Sun Lamp for Cats

You love the sun. All cats do. But what if the windows in your house just don't let in enough light, or you're living far away from the sunny side of town? Just flip a switch on your Sharper Claw AutoSol™ Sun Lamp for Cats, and the sun will come up every day in your neighborhood as you bask in 2000 watts of realistic artificial sunlight. It'll be hard to believe you're not on the Riviera!

Netscratch

File Claws   Stare   Go Hunting   So Many Options   Window on Birds

 Back to Sleep
 Forward To Food
 Home Turf
 Shred It
 Relax
 Open One Eye
 Open Can
 Pounce
 Find Toys
 Stop & Nap

Location: www.publishers-clawinghouse.cat

What's to Eat? | What's Comfy? | Dogless Sites | Mouse Search | Other Cats | Soft Laps

PUBLISHERS CLAWING HOUSE ONLINE SWEEPSTAKES

Because you are the **49800099** cat to visit this web site, you are now a semi-quarter-partial-alternative finalist in our Publishers Clawing House Sweepstakes. You definitely* win the following:

1 Grand Prize—A lifetime supply of your choice of cat food

2 Runner-Up Prizes—Sterling silver or gold-plated food and water bowls

3 Semifinal Prizes—Space-age automatic litter boxes

You Could Be a Winner Like Basil and Iggy!!!!!!!!

Here's what you need to do to claim your prizes:

1. Select the magazines you want:
   Martha Mewart's Living
   US Mews and World Report
   HairBall
   Mewsweek
   Mouse and Garden
   Good Mousekeeping

2. Because you're so close to winning, type in the name of your all-time favorite cat food—a food so wonderful you'd like to get a lifetime supply: [   ]

3. Since we're sure you'll be a winner, select now your preferred precious metal for the food and water bowl you'll receive:
   Sterling Silver
   Gold-Plated

4. Since you'll no doubt be a winner, select now the color of automatic litter box you would like us to ship to you:
   Persian White
   Bombay Black
   Colorful Calico

5. Fill in the necessary information (your name, address, and your human's credit card numbers)

   [   ]

6. Watch TV after the Super Water Dish. Ed McMalayan and Dick Clawk may come to your house, scratch at the door, and award YOU a lifetime supply of your choice of cat food!

   ENTER ME NOW!

   *may have already been selected to be eligible to

Note: Although you do not have to buy any magazines to win, accidental deletions of those entries forwarded WITHOUT magazine orders have been known to occur. Why take a chance when you could . . . WIN A LIFETIME SUPPLY OF YOUR FAVORITE CAT FOOD!

Don't just sit there, enter NOW, and wait for the Prize Patrol to scratch on YOUR door!

File Claws   **Stare**   **Go Hunting**   **So Many Options**   **Window on Birds**

Back to Sleep | Forward To Food | Home Turf | Shred It | Relax | Open One Eye | Open Can | Pounce | Find Toys | Stop & Nap

Location: www.litter-bearing.cat

What's to Eat?   **What's Comfy?**   **Dogless Sites**   **Mouse Search**   **Other Cats**   **Soft Laps**

Litter-Bearing

Dealing with Troublemakers:

When carrying them around by the scruff of the neck isn't enough
Click <u>HERE</u> to chat!

Today's MotherCat Chats

Ask an Expert
What does a newborn's mew actually mean? What's the best furniture for sharpening those little kitten claws?

PREGNANCY & LABOR
- Picking the best place to give birth—used towels vs. clean sweaters
- Using pregnancy to manipulate your human to get even better food and treatment

KITTEN CARE
- Licking clean—proper tongue techniques
- Taking your kittens with you—mastering the "nape of the neck" carry

HOTLINKS:
The La Lechat League

KITTEN DEVELOPMENT
- New developmental toys—red, black, and white mice
- Selecting the correct half dead mouse for your kitten's hunting education

AUDIO FUN—FURRY TAILS

Hear the story of "<u>Little Furry Riding Hood</u>" as she takes the trip to Grandma's and encounters the Big Bad Dog!

File Claws   Stare   Go Hunting   So Many Options   Window on Birds

 Back to Sleep
 Forward To Food
 Home Turf
 Shred It
 Relax
 Open One Eye
 Open Can
 Pounce
 Find Toys
Stop & Nap

Location: **www.transvesticat.cat**

What's to Eat?   What's Comfy?   Dogless Sites   Mouse Search   Other Cats   Soft Laps

Transvest icat

When You're a Dog on the Outside, but a Cat on the Inside

Chat

Today's Chat: Meet Rex, aka the Divine Miss C, three-time Miss Feline America, as she shares her secrets for purring, meowing, hissing, and arching the back.

Visit the RealCat Catalog at www.real.cat
for dogs who want to add what nature forgot

See our new collection of:
- faux whiskers
- ears
- fluffy tails

Books

Transvesticat reviews *Man's Best Friend No More: Being Your Own Best Feline Friend*

Spring Semester Online Courses for New Transvesticats

Finicky 101

Ignoring 201

Slinking 301

Register ENTER

for the Drag Dog Ball and witness the crowning of Miss Feline America, who will reign as Queen of the Transvesticats for the next year!

File Claws   Stare   Go Hunting   So Many Options   Window on Birds

 Back to Sleep Forward To Food IF FOUND CALL: Home Turf Shred It Relax Open One Eye Open Can Pounce Find Toys Stop & Nap

Location: **www.cat-navy.cat**

What's to Eat?   What's Comfy?   Dogless Sites   Mouse Search   Other Cats   Soft Laps

Be all that you can be, if you really want to bother . . .

JOIN THE CAT-NAVY!

JOBS IN THE FLEET
Click here for more information about a wide variety of Cat-Navy jobs. Hunt rats and mice from many lands. Whatever your speciality, the Cat-Navy has a great opportunity for you.

WORLDWIDE TRAVEL
Ready to try your luck? The Cat-Navy has exciting jobs in the most exotic places. When you live on a ship, you can see the world without ever leaving home. Mate with native females in every port. Check this section to see where the Cat-Navy may take you today.

WHAT'S NEW IN THE NAVY
Discover what's new in the Cat-Navy. Latest report: Fresh fish now offered at every meal.

BE A SHIP'S CAT!

NEXT SCHEDULED SHIP LEAVES IN 10 DAYS

Sign up now!

Enlist Me!

JOIN THE FEW, THE PROUD, THE SLIGHTLY DAMP.

Cat-Navy: It's not just a job, it's an opportunity to take naps in many exotic climes.

File Claws   Stare   Go Hunting   So Many Options   Window on Birds

Back to Sleep | Forward To Food | Home Turf | Shred It | Relax | Open One Eye | Open Can | Pounce | Find Toys | Stop & Nap

Location: www.psycatology.cat

What's to Eat? | What's Comfy? | Dogless Sites | Mouse Search | Other Cats | Soft Laps

PSYCATOLOGY-NET
Where You'll Learn to Understand the Inner "Mew"

FAQs

- How can you fulfill the needs of your inner kitten?

- The hallucinatory effects of paper bags: Why do they appear to be fascinating caves or dens?

- Kneading—useful bed-site preparation or mother fixation?

- Do you have bi-polecat disorder?

NEW FEATURE
Whiskers and Paws That Twitch in Your Sleep—Peering Into the World of Cat Dreams

SMART LINK
Crazy Cats Anonymous:
For Cats Who Get the Urge to Tear Wildly Around the House for No Good Reason

ONLINE CHAT
Tonight's Discussion:
MOUSE REMORSE—Should we feel sorry for our prey?

INTERACTIVE QUIZ
Who Am I? Reestablishing Your Identity After Neutering.
Click here to take our Interactive Quiz.

A best-seller for 40 weeks!
Calicodependent No More
Click to order.

Back to Sleep | Forward To Food | Home Turf | Shred It | Relax | Open One Eye | Open Can | Pounce | Find Toys | Stop & Nap

Location: www.catortions.cat

| What's to Eat? | What's Comfy? | Dogless Sites | Mouse Search | Other Cats | Soft Laps |

"101 Ways to Put Your Paw in Your Mouth"
Order your copy of this best seller today!

Catortions

FAQs
- How can I clean the top of my head with just my tongue?
- What if I land on just three legs instead of all four?
- How many legs should I properly land on when bungee jumping?
- What's more important in jumping: distance or grace?
- What do I need to know before using a kite as a hang glider?

New Photo DOWNLOADS!
Download these photos of ten strange new sleeping positions guaranteed to contort even the most flexible cat!

FLYING CATORTIONS
Out of the Frying Pan—How to Look Before You Leap

From Hard Surfaces to Soft Surfaces: Dos and Don'ts

Back to Sleep   Forward To Food   Home Turf   Shred It   Relax   Open One Eye   Open Can   Pounce   Find Toys   Stop & Nap

Location: www.good-old-cats.cat

What's to Eat?   What's Comfy?   Dogless Sites   Mouse Search   Other Cats   Soft Laps

WWW.GOODOLDCATS Celebrating Redneck Cats!
You know you're a redneck cat if...

- You have a gun rack on your litter box.

- Instead of hissing at dogs, you spit tobacco juice at them.

- You scrounged your cat toys out of an old refrigerator in the yard.

- Your fur is teased so much that you can't get through most cat doors.

- You prefer kudzu to catnip.

- You have two litter boxes, but one spends all of its time in the yard up on cinder blocks.

- Your kibble is made by Red Man.

- As a kitten, you thought that a smoker's hack always naturally followed a "meow."

- Your water bowl is an open six-pack.

Click here for more "You Know You're a Redneck Cat" sayings.

Meet Bubba, one of our chat-room regulars, in GoodOldCat-Chat CLICK HERE to CHAT

GoodOldCat Classifieds: Wanted—tickets to Monster Litter Box Show. Click here for more . . .

SIGN UP NOW! Join the redneck cats today and receive a bail bond up to $5,000, free fur tattoos, and a package of toothpicks.

File Claws   Stare   Go Hunting   So Many Options   Window on Birds

| Back to Sleep | Forward To Food | Home Turf | Shred It | Relax | Open One Eye | Open Can | Pounce | Find Toys | Stop & Nap |

Location: www.MeowdioNet.cat

| What's to Eat? | What's Comfy? | Dogless Sites | Mouse Search | Other Cats | Soft Laps |

~*MeowdioNet*~
The Audio Network for Cats

Sporting Events

7:00 P.M. EST—Baltimore Oriyowls vs. the New York Yankats
7:00 P.M. CST—San Diego Pawdres vs. the Seattle Meowiners
10:00 P.M. EST—World Tinfoil-Ball Finals
(Sponsored by Cat Sports Online)

MeowdioNet Jukebox

Click to hear your favorite tunes . . .
Cat with No Name
50 Ways to Eat Your Kibble
I Scratched the Sheriff

Audio Book Clips

Hear an audio clip from the new book *10 Smart Things Cats Can Do to Drive People Crazy* as read by the author, radio personality Dr. Laura Pussinger.

Deepcat Chowdown discusses his new book, *The Seven Spiritual Laws of Laziness.*

Listen to Chapter One of the best-selling self-help book, *Calicodependent No More,* as read by actress Meow Farrow.

DEEPCAT CHOWDOWN
THE SEVEN SPIRITUAL LAWS OF LAZINESS

Today's Audio Events

Live chat with Julia Kitten, world renowned chef, on how to make a great "Mouse Souffle" (Sponsored by Chaute Cuisine/Gourmet Cats Online)

Hear home decorating maven Martha Mewart's ideas on how to turn your Persian carpet into a "purrfect" shag with just your claws and a glue gun. (Sponsored by Martha Mewart's Shredding)

Speeches and Press Conferences

Weight-loss guru Richard Mittens introduces his groundbreaking new diet program, "Squeal a Meal" (Sponsored by the Fat Cat Weight Loss Centers)

Ross Purr-oh, frequent Presidential candidate, presents his latest mewsings. (Sponsored by Ross Purr-oh for President)

Back to Sleep | Forward To Food | Home Turf | Shred It | Relax | Open One Eye | Open Can | Pounce | Find Toys | Stop & Nap

Location: **www.nyt-books.cat**

What's to Eat? | What's Comfy? | Dogless Sites | Mouse Search | Other Cats | Soft Laps

The New Yowl Times
REVIEW OF BOOKS

Books

"WHERE TO SCRATCH UP WHAT TO READ"

The New Yowl Times
Book Review
Focus on Cat Books

Number of Cat Books Currently on Display at Bookstore Checkout Counters

5 3 0 7 9 2 3 9 5 0 9 9 2

Bedtime Stories for Cats by Leigh Anne Jasheway. Puts a twist on several classic fairy tales, complete with heroic cats and happy endings. Has too many human characters, but those depicted are relatively unannoying. Overall, a very enjoyable read. ($9.95)

In the Company of Cats: A Tribute to the Feline. Edited by Linda Sunshine. Although this book is designed for humans, the pictures and almost all of the quotations are properly flattering. The book is a useful reminder of the appropriate deference humans must pay to cats. ($15.00)

Hero Cats by Eric Swanson. When foolish humans get in trouble, who will save them? Cats, of course. Includes color photos of many heroic and fearless hero cats. ($14.95)

Cat Home Alone by Regen Dennis. Provides humans with a number of good suggestions for making us more comfortable and entertained. Although we do not generally believe in any toy made by humans, the toy included is certainly one of the better ones. ($10.95)

Cat's Cradle by Kurt Vonnegut. A misleadingly titled load of mishmash that provides absolutely no useful information on bringing up kittens. ($6.99)

The Cats' House by Bob Walker. Shows a human how to improve any house by constructing cat skyways, complete with stairs, ramps, and special windows. Get this book into the hands of any human handyman! ($16.95)

A Passion for Kittens by J.C. Suares. A collection of the cutest kitten pictures ever taken. And the accompanying quotations are unusually insightful, considering they come from humans. ($10.95)

The Rules for Cats: The Secret to Getting Free Catnip for Life by Leigh Anne Jasheway. Provides a good summary of the basic rules for dealing with humans. Interestingly, a variation of this book, designed for human females seeking mates, has also been produced. ($6.95)

Like Cats and Dogs by Tanya McKinnon and Gayatri Patnaik. A description of the relatively enlightened humans who are owned by cats, as well as the dimwit humans who live with dogs. Also explores the bizarre world of "bi-nines"—those weird humans who have sense enough to enjoy cats, yet inexplicably like dogs, too. ($19.95)

Back to Sleep | Forward To Food | IF FOUND CALL: Home Turf | Shred It | Relax | Open One Eye | Open Can | Pounce | Find Toys | Stop & Nap

Location: www.muscle-tail.cat

What's to Eat?　|　What's Comfy?　|　Dogless Sites　|　Mouse Search　|　Other Cats　|　Soft Laps

FITNESS

Improving Your Fitness Between Naps

- The Stroll to Your Bowl: Any Kind of Walking Will Improve Your Health!
- Having Trouble Finding the Incentive to Do Your Wind Sprints? Tease a Dog (Here's How)!
- Vertical Push-ups: The Latest Rage

INSIGHTS

Find Out What Your Tail Says About You—
Click on the tail that resembles yours.

MUSCLE TAIL

For Muscle-and-Tail-Building Enthusiasts

DOWNLOADS

Latest Competition Techniques:

- Starching Your Tail: Pros and Cons
- Visualization Methods: How Just Thinking About That Dog/Vet/ Neighbor Cat Can Improve Your Tail Fluffing Performance
- Competition Tips from the Recent Winner of the Mr. Biggest-Fur-in-the-Universe Competition, Arlynx Schwarzenfuzzy

Get Every Hair Standing on End: Great New Fluffing Techniques

Back to Sleep

Forward To Food

Home Turf

Shred It

Relax

Open One Eye

Open Can

Pounce

Find Toys

Stop & Nap

Location: www.dr-laura.cat

What's to Eat?   What's Comfy?   Dogless Sites   Mouse Search   Other Cats   Soft Laps

THE OFFICIAL SITE FOR

DR. LAURA PUSSINGER

GO SCRATCH ON THE SOFA

Hear Dr. Laura's Theme Song: "I've Got a New Cattitude!"

Dr. Laura Pussinger is the most popular psycatherapist in cyberspace. She brings morality and order back to the wild kingdom of cat life.

Favorite Audio Clips:

Dr. Laura Pussinger blasts a caller who asks, "Should I agree to mate with him solely on the basis of his size and tail height?"

FAQ

- Why can't I have kittens even if I can't afford cat food?
- Why do I keep picking love 'em and leave 'em tomcats?
- Is there ever a time when it's wrong to relieve my anxieties by destroying furniture?
- Why am I fatally attracted to calicoes in distress?
- Is it okay for a female to sit idly by while two males fight over her? If so, how broadly can she smile without appearing too pleased?

ON SALE NOW!
Dr. Laura Pussinger's New Book:

10 Smart Things Cats Can Do to Drive People Crazy!

CATWORLD'S LARGEST BOOKSELLER ONLINE
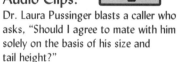
BarncatandNoble.cat

Netscratch

File Claws   Stare   Go Hunting   So Many Options   Window on Birds

  Back to Sleep   **Forward To Food** **Home Turf**   **Shred It**   **Relax**   **Open One Eye**   **Open Can**   **Pounce**   **Find Toys**   **Stop & Nap**

Location: www.opurra.cat

What's to Eat?   What's Comfy?   Dogless Sites   Mouse Search   Other Cats   Soft Laps

Schedules

Opurra News

Your guide to the best international back-fence yowling

Reviews

By our armchair opurra fanatic, Eduardo Inderrieden-Tabbyworth III . . .

Select the performance schedules for all the major backyard fences throughout the world including:

☐ Catnegie Hall
☐ The Meowtropolitan Opera
☐ Chicago Yowlyric Opera
☐ La Yowlla in Milan

Profile of "The Three Yowlers"

Placatio Domingo, José Cateras, and Luciano Pavarateater

Catmen by Bizet
The Burmese of Seville
The Magic Foodbowl
Toscat
Die Flederkatze
Madame Catterfly
Der Rosencatelier
Die Cätterdämmerung
Paggliacat

This Week's Highlighted FAQ: How can I best dodge shoes and other critical impedimenta thrown by "artistic ignoramuses"?

46

File Claws   Stare   Go Hunting   So Many Options   Window on Birds

 Back to Sleep
 Forward To Food
 Home Turf
 Shred It
 Relax
 Open One Eye
 Open Can
 Pounce
 Find Toys
Stop & Nap

Location: www.nip.cat

| What's to Eat? | What's Comfy? | Dogless Sites | Mouse Search | Other Cats | Soft Laps |

'Nip

Getting 'Nipped

- Grow Your Own—Tips for the 'Niphead
- Mexican Airless versus Scottish Folded
- The Ultimate 'Nip: Meowie Wowie

Special Report
How to Spot a 'Nip Narc

Download Recipes

- 'Nip Nachos
- 'Nip Brownies

CATNIP

FAQ

* What's more potent: fresh or dried?
* What should you do when they're bogarting the 'nip?
* How do you tell if your 'nip is cut with parsley?
* Where's the best place to store your stash?

File Claws   Stare   Go Hunting   So Many Options   Window on Birds

Back to Sleep | Forward To Food | Home Turf | Shred It | Relax | Open One Eye | Open Can | Pounce | Find Toys | Stop & Nap

Location: www.kitten-welfare-league.cat

What's to Eat? | What's Comfy? | Dogless Sites | Mouse Search | Other Cats | Soft Laps

Kitten Welfare League
Providing Aid for Kittens Around the World

This is Peaches.

Peaches lives indoors in the badlands of Montana. In this arid land—where houses are sealed against the extremes of heat and cold—few household pests can survive. As a result—Peaches is growing up alone in her house—without hope of any creatures to catch and play with. She is growing up mouse-deprived . . .

But you can help. By supporting the KWL and sponsoring a kitten like Peaches, you can help kittens living in challenging environments—kittens in homes

that have no mice, no rats, no vermin—those things that most cats take for granted for their entertainment and well-being.

Won't you take just a moment to join us in our continuing effort to help these kittens by making your electronic pledge now? Your support, which you can show by clicking the box to the left, will insure that a rubber mouse is sent immediately to a kitten just like Peaches.

Won't you please help me ? Or you can surf away. The choice is yours . . .

YES, I WANT TO HELP! HERE'S MY DONATION FOR PEACHES!

I'M HEARTLESS. LET PEACHES GO MOUSELESS.

Netscratch

File Claws   Stare   Go Hunting   So Many Options   Window on Birds

Back to Sleep | Forward To Food | Home Turf | Shred It | Relax | Open One Eye | Open Can | Pounce | Find Toys | Stop & Nap

Location: www.dining-out.cat

What's to Eat?   What's Comfy?   Dogless Sites   Mouse Search   Other Cats   Soft Laps

Dining Out Food Reviews

Featuring famous *Washington Scratching Post* food critic,

Phyllis Richcat

Dead Lobster

🐾🐾🐾🐾🐾

The trademark red dumpster offers a veritable nirvana of tasty treats. And when the special All-You-Can-Eat Buffet is ordered, there are always plenty of scraps of fried scrod and tiny shrimp for all. Ship ahoy!

GFC
Colonel Blanders Greasy Fried Chicken

🐾🐾🐾

Buried under mounds of greasy GFC paper products in the dumpster, you'll find a blizzard of bones with wonderfully tasty meat bits. (Just don't eat the bones themselves!) It's chicken that's "Fur-Lickin' Good!"

the Feline Garden

🐾🐾🐾🐾

The Feline Garden's dumpster features a delightful mixture of spaghetti, meat sauce, and ricotta. If you're lucky, you might even enjoy the house special, chicken parmigiana. Meowto bene!

TACO CAT

🐾

Pathetic meat scraps, lots of grease, and way too much spice are all this dumpster offers for the sensitive feline palate. Time to vamoose, amigo!

In YOUR Neighborhood

The Hashimoto Family: Travel to the Far East has never been finer than a visit to the Hashimoto family trash can. Mysterious but most interesting raw fish dishes appear frequently here. Ah, so delicious!

The Hashimoto Family
Click HERE for Directions

The Matthews Family: Standard boring middle-American cuisine is all you'll find in this trash can. Sparse pickings, including lots of white bread crusts and drippings from the Jello mold. Aside from that, what little there is looks like it was scraped off the side of the refrigerator. Don't waste your time.

File Claws   Stare   Go Hunting   So Many Options   Window on Birds

 Back to Sleep Forward To Food Home Turf Shred It Relax Open One Eye Open Can Pounce Find Toys Stop & Nap

Location: **www.pbs.cat**

| What's to Eat? | What's Comfy? | Dogless Sites | Mouse Search | Other Cats | Soft Laps |

Masterpuss Theater's "Indoors Outdoors"

A nine-part *Masterpuss Theater* special series on the private lives of the privileged indoor cats and the scrappy, less fortunate outdoor cats that share their domicile.

Live from Lincat Center

Sir Neville Manx Conducting the London Philharmonicat in Tchaivokscat's *Third Symphony*

National Geographicat Presents:

"Mysterious Man," a look at the strange, mysterious, and unpredictable behaviors of the elusive "Man."

PBS online

Pussycat Broadcasting System

The Seven Spiritual Laws of Laziness

Join spiritual expert Deepcat Chowdown as he talks about his newest book and how you can achieve truly spiritual laziness by following his principles.

Pledge Week

The Three Yowlers

Join famous yowlers Placatio Domingo, José Cateras and Luciano Pavarateater as they perform your favorites!

Featured This Month

Just for Kids!

- Siamese Street

- Mr. Rogers' Territory

TRUE RED, WHITE, AND MEW PATRIOTS

AN ONLINE NEWSMAGAZINE FOR REAL AMERICATS

 ## LATEST CONSPIRACIES

- Neutering: Forced Population-Control Plot Directed by an Unholy Alliance of Nazis, Commies, and Federal Bureaucrats!

- Worldwide Disasters: A Plot to Interfere with Our Naps?

- Catnip: Natural Treat or Federal Mind-Control Program?

- Why the Government's Attempts to Silence Morris the Cat Sent Him into Hiding

Morris, undercover in camouflage

 ## TRUE NEWS

New Evidence Reveals That the Black Animal-Control Vans Are Jointly Controlled by the United Nations and the Estate of Marlin Perkins

Why the Government Wants to Take Away Your Claws—Fighting for Your Right to Bare Paws!

Why the Government Won't Tell You the Truth About Your Kibble

 SIGN UP TO FIND TRUE RED, WHITE, AND MEW MEETINGS IN YOUR AREA

File Claws   **Stare**   **Go Hunting**   **So Many Options**   **Window on Birds**

 Back to Sleep
 Forward To Food
 Home Turf
 Shred It
 Relax
 Open One Eye
 Open Can
 Pounce
 Find Toys
 Stop & Nap

Location: **www.cat-lady.cat** ▼

| **What's to Eat?** | **What's Comfy?** | **Dogless Sites** | **Mouse Search** | **Other Cats** | **Soft Laps** |

Cat-Lady

The Web Site for Cats Living in Households with 20+ Cats

New at the Web Site!
When You All Look Alike!
Ways to Get Your Cat Lady to Pay More Attention to YOU!

Number of Cats in the Average Cat Lady's House   24

Frequently Asked Questions
- How can I get a good place at the dish?
- How can I convince my cat lady to get her Social Security paid in cans of Nine Lives?

DOWNLOAD NOW!!
Audio tips on what to do and where to hide if the Health Department shows up.

THE CAT-LADY-ULATOR

Enter Square Footage of Your Cat lady's House/Apartment   [ ]   **ENTER**

Optimum number of cats per square foot
[ ]

 Watch the **Fishing Channel** 24 hours a day on cable

Indoor Fishin'

Let Cap'n Jack Find You the **BIG ONE!!**

"The best aquarium charter excursions!"
—*Catbait 'n' Tackle* magazine

AquaCat Fishing Gear

The Only Thing to Wear for the Well-Dressed Aqua Cat

RECOMMENDED BY JACQUES CATSEAU, UNDERSEA DIVER!

AquariumMaster Fishing Boats: Indoor Fishin' reviews the latest model

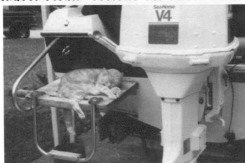

What's Biting This Week?

- Using your tail as an emergency lure
- Practicing your casting technique when your human is taking a bath
- Your best source of bait: the refrigerator freezer
- Warning signs of a piranha
- Beware the dry aquarium: spotting the python before it's too late

Download Team Sink-Fishing Techniques from the Experts

Back to Sleep | Forward To Food | Home Turf | Shred It | Relax | Open One Eye | Open Can | Pounce | Find Toys | Stop & Nap

Location: www.catinentalairlines.cat

What's to Eat? | What's Comfy? | Dogless Sites | Mouse Search | Other Cats | Soft Laps

Catinental Airlines

TravelCat Online
For the Few Cats Who Actually *Like* to Travel

What's New!

- **New addition to Economy Kibble Class service: Complimentary liver snacks!**
- **Now! Seven Catalina Island to Catalan Province flights daily!**
- **Check out our daily nonstop jet service to the best fishing locations!**

Book Tickets:
Click to select class:

 Premier Caviar

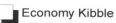 Economy Kibble

 Cat Carrier

This Month's Catinental Travel Close-up:
Your Hotel Room Can Be an Amusement Park!

- Pull out tissues from the built-in boxes—hours of fun! (And the maid will always bring you more!)
- Hotel carpeting: Your complimentary claw sharpener
- Pillow mints make excellent cat hockey pucks

Sign up for our Frequent Meow-er Program

- 5,000 miles = Your own smoked salmon
- 10,000 miles = Your own home fishtank, with fish

Free Software!

Click HERE to download TravelCat TravelPlanner 2000! Plan travel so it doesn't interfere with naps, meals, and playtime.

File Claws   **Stare**   **Go Hunting**   **So Many Options**   **Window on Birds**

Back to Sleep | Forward To Food | Home Turf | IF FOUND CALL: | Shred It | Relax | Open One Eye | Open Can | Pounce | Find Toys | Stop & Nap

Location: www.x-terior-files.cat

What's to Eat?   **What's Comfy?**   **Dogless Sites**   **Mouse Search**   **Other Cats**   **Soft Laps**

THE (X)TERIOR FILES
The Truth Is Outside the House Somewhere

The Web's Most Popular FAQ on the Hit TV Show, *The X-terior Files*

EXCLUSIVE VIDEO DOWNLOAD!!

Download these exclusive real-life video clips of what is actually kept in the mysterious "Kennel 51"

TODAY IN THE CHAT ROOM:

Who is Catnip Man? What strange power does he have over other cats?

This week's* questions:

X What did Meowlder see in that cardboard box?

X When Meowlder was a kitten, was his littermate sister taken away by unknown humans?

X Why does it always seem like the Feline Bureau of Investigation is out to get Meowlder and Scullycat?

X What is the shadowy organization that prowls the streets, causing cats who have no licenses to disappear?

X Why, just when we're about to get a good look at something scary, is it always obscured by fog and bright lights?

X Will Meowlder and Scullycat ever get around to mating?

* In all honesty, these are every week's discussion questions.

File Claws   Stare   Go Hunting   So Many Options   Window on Birds

   Back to Sleep / Forward To Food / Home Turf   Shred It   Relax   Open One Eye   Open Can   Pounce   Find Toys   Stop & Nap

Location: www.sophisticat_aristocat.cat

What's to Eat? | What's Comfy? | Dogless Sites | Mouse Search | Other Cats | Soft Laps

Sophisticat Aristocat

SPECIAL REPORT!
When You Have to Board:
The 20 Best Boarding Kennels

Around the House:
Good Help Is Hard to Find: Ten Pointers on Hiring the Best Humans

This Week on the Web:
- Gold vs. Platinum: What's In for Bowls This Year
- Have Your Butler Do Your Spraying for You
- Where to Find the Fluffiest Nap Cushions
- Caviar and Catnip: The Kibble of Kings

Fashion: Diamonds Are a Cat's Best Friend (So Lose That Rhinestone Collar)

Society: Purebred Parties: A Look at the Social Lives of the Better Cats

Travel: Where the Rockefelines and Vandercats Are Vacationing This Year

Catting About:
Catalan Province Vs. Catalina Island: Where Shall You Summer?

sponsored by
Dean Litter and Company
Your Investment Partner Through All Your Nine Lives

| Back to Sleep | Forward To Food | Home Turf | Shred It | Relax | Open One Eye | Open Can | Pounce | Find Toys | Stop & Nap |

Location: www.sharper-claw.cat/health

What's to Eat?　　What's Comfy?　　Dogless Sites　　Mouse Search　　Other Cats　　Soft Laps

THE SHARPER CLAW®
online catalog

Search for

Health & More
Home Sweet Home
Great Outdoors
Snack Time
Comfort Zone

Scratch <u>HERE</u> to order!!

Click <u>HERE</u> for the "Home Sweet Home" collection to make your life more convenient!

Tongueomatic™ Fur Licker, for Beautiful Fur the Easy Way

Every day, the same old thing—lick, lick, lick your fur. But why waste precious nap time when you can use the Sharper Claw Tongueomatic™ Fur Licker? Its hundreds of raised dots quickly clean your fur and give you a relaxing massage. Even better than Mom used to do when you were a kitten. (Batteries not included.)

Sharper Claw Automatic Claw Sharpener™

Tired of sharpening your claws on the same old furniture and listening to your human's ridiculous shrieks? Our signature Sharper Claw Automatic Claw Sharpener™ uses precision stainless-steel blades to bring your claws to a razor's edge. A Sharper Claw exclusive and perennial favorite!

Summonizer 2000™ Electronic Human Caller

You want your human to come, but don't want to strain your voice. Not a problem with the Summonizer 2000™ Electronic Human Caller. Just prerecord your call with the microphone and you're ready to blast your yowl into the next county with stadium-quality speakers. Deluxe premium ear plugs are included for your protection.

Back to Sleep | Forward To Food | IF FOUND CALL: Home Turf | Shred It | Relax | Open One Eye | Open Can | Pounce | Find Toys | Stop & Nap

Location: www.birds.cat

What's to Eat? | What's Comfy? | Dogless Sites | Mouse Search | Other Cats | Soft Laps

Blue Jays and Mockingbirds— Attackers from the Air: Mounting the Proper Anti-Air Defense

All About BIRDS

DOWNLOAD

"Who me?" and ten more great excuses you can use to explain why the parakeet isn't in his cage anymore.

The Hunt for Red Octoberfest: Searching for Tasty Cardinals in the Fall

ASK the EXPERT

This week's question: How can I plant those leftover feathers in the dog's mouth?

DINNER-CAM

This week, the camera focuses on: "Sparrows— Quick Snacks of the Bird World."

The Bird Word— Audio Downloads: Hear poet Meowya Angelou reading her masterpiece *I Know Why the Caged Bird Doesn't Sing*

File Claws   Stare   Go Hunting   So Many Options   Window on Birds

 Back to Sleep
 Forward To Food
 Home Turf
 Shred It
 Relax
 Open One Eye
 Open Can
 Pounce
 Find Toys
 Stop & Nap

Location: www.toasty.cat

What's to Eat? | What's Comfy? | Dogless Sites | Mouse Search | Other Cats | Soft Laps

Comfy Asbestos Blankets

Ever wake up to find your fur smoking? Our asbestos blankets are soft to the touch and kind to sensitive noses, yet protect you from excess temperatures while still allowing that lovely heat to come through.

Goggles

End dry eyes with these special goggles, based on the same technology humans use to protect themselves when fighting oil-well fires. Held on with a padded strap that won't muss your fur.

Fur Singe Restorer Cream

For those occasions when you overdo it, our cream will condition overly dried fur and return it to kittenlike softness. Just apply with your tongue.

TOASTY CAT CATALOG

Fireplace accessories for the cat who likes to lie as close to the fire as possible

 PLACE ORDER

Toasty Cat Heater

How many cats have suffered the heartbreak of seeing a fireplace in a new home, only to learn that it's artificial? Not a problem with our add-on heater. With settings ranging from "lightly roasted" to "raging inferno," you're sure to find the pleasing warmth you crave.

Famous Toasty Cat's Thermometer Readings:

Temperature in Front of Morris's Fireplace: 125 degrees

Temperature in Front of Madonna's Cat's Fireplace: 192 degrees

Temperature in Front of Al Gore's Cat's Fireplace: 58 degrees

File Claws   Stare   Go Hunting   So Many Options   Window on Birds

Back to Sleep | Forward To Food | Home Turf | Shred It | Relax | Open One Eye | Open Can | Pounce | Find Toys | Stop & Nap

Location: www.chaute_cuisine.cat

What's to Eat? | What's Comfy? | Dogless Sites | Mouse Search | Other Cats | Soft Laps

Chaute Cuisine
Gourmet Cats Online

LATEST UPDATES

 100 Exotic, Attractive, and Exciting Things to Eat Around the House

 Kitchen Tables: The All-You-Can-Eat Smorgasbord You Might Be Overlooking

 Demands for Food Even the Stupidest Human Can't Ignore

 The Miracle Source of Fresh Water That Never Runs Dry

Number of Cats Eating Right Now
939972639

HOTLINKS

Morris Online

How I Parlayed "Finicky" Eating into Fame and Fortune

"We Love Grass" Web Site
Just the Thing to Eat When You Can't Believe You Ate the Whole Thing

NEW DOWNLOADS

More great games to play with food you don't like:
• Ultimate Friskees
• Pureena Cat Hockey

FAQ

➤ What are the best ways to convince humans that they haven't fed me, even if they just did?

➤ Why does the food in someone else's bowl always taste better?

➤ Do chicken bones stolen out of the trash taste better when eaten under the sofa or on the bed?

➤ Is it more polite to start with the head or the tail?

➤ When should I chew versus swallowing whole?

➤ From dry to soft to salmon: How can I get my human to upgrade my food selections?

File Claws   Stare   Go Hunting   So Many Options   Window on Birds

 Back to Sleep | Forward To Food | Home Turf | Shred It | Relax | Open One Eye | Open Can | Pounce | Find Toys | Stop & Nap

Location: www.meowter-trend.cat

What's to Eat? | What's Comfy? | Dogless Sites | Mouse Search | Other Cats | Soft Laps

---

This Site Is a 1998 Winner of the Scratchy Award

MEOWTOR TREND
online

BUYING GUIDE

Meowdi
Catillac
TOYOWLTA

Furrari

In this issue:

- Meowtor Trend Compares Back Window Shelf Space Size and Comfort in the Top Ten Cars
- An Exclusive Look at the New Designs for the Space Under the Gas Pedal on the '99 Models
- Seat-to-Window Ratios in Sport Utility Vehicles

Driving Lesson

This Week: Can You Really Teach Humans How to Drive?

Hotlinks

- Newsgroup: alt.racing.meowzda
- *Cat and Driver* magazine

SPECIAL REPORT

PURRSCHE

File Claws   Stare   Go Hunting   So Many Options   Window on Birds

  Back to Sleep   Forward To Food   Home Turf   Shred It   Relax   Open One Eye   Open Can   Pounce   Find Toys   Stop & Nap

Location: **www.vegecat.cat**

What's to Eat?   What's Comfy?   Dogless Sites   Mouse Search   Other Cats   Soft Laps

Winner: Holisticat Site of the Week

FAQ

How can I keep the mice in my house at bay, even if they know I won't eat them?

How can I throw up something I've eaten if I decide I don't like it?

Live Plant-Cam

Vege-cat

For the Vegetarian Cat

This Week at Vege-cat Online

- Grass: The miraculous natural laxative
- Hydrolyzed animal proteins and other cat-food ingredients that say "meat"
- Ten tasty tulip recipes
- Floral displays: An instant salad bar

Hot Links

The Official "Just Say No to Catnip" Site

Poinsettia Poison Control Hotline

Netscratch

File Claws   Stare   Go Hunting   So Many Options   Window on Birds

 Back to Sleep   Forward To Food   IF FOUND CALL: Home Turf   Shred It   Relax   Open One Eye   Open Can   Pounce   Find Toys   Stop & Nap

Location: **www.scratchingpost.cat**

What's to Eat?   What's Comfy?   Dogless Sites   Mouse Search   Other Cats   Soft Laps

Special Report:
Catnip Lobbyists Accused of Giving Congresscats Tongue Baths

The Washington Scratching Post

Select a Section   go   **site index | search | help**

 **Style**

Featuring the Reliable Purr and Miss Manxers

Meow Jones:
Average Climbs on Strength of Mew Chip Stocks

Metro: Former Mayor Marion Birman found OD'd on Catnip in City Hotel Room with Trio of Persians . . . Again

Democats and Republicats Fail to Agree on Mouse Redistribution, Engage in Paw Pointing

Party leaders, meeting in a neutral backyard, failed again to reach agreement on a new formula for redistribution of mice. Negotiations continue, but are hindered by mutual accusations of catty behavior. Read Full Story...

Photo: Neshan Naltcatchayan

International/National:
- Anti-Neutering Supporters Prowl Washington Streets
- New South American Catnip Appearing on U.S. Streets
- Russian Blues "Blue" over Low Caviar Harvest
- Allegations Continue Regarding Socks' White House Relationships

Business:
- Catinental Air Lines to Merge with Air Catnada
- Cheap Rubber Mice Imported from Southeast Asia Flooding United Cats of America Markets

File Claws   Stare   Go Hunting   So Many Options   Window on Birds

 Back to Sleep   Forward To Food   Home Turf   Shred It   Relax   Open One Eye   Open Can   Pounce   Find Toys   Stop & Nap

Location: www.spicecats.cat

What's to Eat? | What's Comfy? | Dogless Sites | Mouse Search | Other Cats | Soft Laps

Auditions!

Spice Cats are looking for new members! If you've got what it takes, click to sign up for your audition to join the Spice Cats. We need cats to try out for the following:

- Smelly Spice
- Scratchy Spice
- Howly Spice
- Shedding Spice
- Spraying Spice

[   ]
[Sign me up!]

FAQ

- What does "Cat Power" really mean and why do the Spice Cats say it incessantly?
- What do the Spice Cats and Milli Vanillacat have in common?

THE SPICE CATS

Lyric Sheet

OK! You asked for it. Here are the formerly undecipherable lyrics of the HIT Spice Cat song, "Wannabe Eating."

Tell you what I'll eat,
what I'll really really eat.
So tell me what you'll eat,
what you'll really really eat.
I wanna I wanna I wanna I wanna
I wanna really really really big salmon
or cod.
If you want to be my human
You gotta stock up on fish.
Keep it comin' faster
Filling up my dish.
If you want to be my human
Just let me rule the house.
Feed me, pet me, love me
Get me a pet mouse.

SPICECATWORLD
THE MOVIE

Back to Sleep

Forward To Food

Home Turf

Shred It

Relax

Open One Eye

Open Can

Pounce

Find Toys

Stop & Nap

Location: **www.alleycat.cat**

What's to Eat?   What's Comfy?   Dogless Sites   Mouse Search   Other Cats   Soft Laps

ALLEYCAT ONLINE
FOR LEAN, MEAN, FELINE FIGHTING MACHINES

THE KING OF THE ALLEY SPEAKS

TERRITORY: GET IT. KEEP IT.

NEW! NEW!

LEARN KUNG MEW: THE SIAMESE ART OF SELF-DEFENSE AND CLEANLINESS

 LIVE ALLEY-CAM

LICK HERE TO SEE A REAL CATFIGHT IN PROGRESS!

FAQ

- TECHNIQUE I: WHY IS A YOWL WORTH A THOUSAND BLOWS?
- TECHNIQUE II: HOW DO YOU PROTECT YOUR NOSE?
- TECHNIQUE III: WHAT'S BETTER, CLAWING OR BITING?
- HOW CAN YOU SERRATE YOUR CLAWS FOR MAXIMUM EFFECT?
- FIRST AID—WHAT IS THE RIGHT WAY TO LICK YOUR WOUNDS?
- POSSUMS VS. RACCOONS—WHICH ARE WORSE?

ALLEYCAT'S TERRITORY MAP-O-MATIC

Enter your zip code and receive a detailed street map showing blocked-off territories as of midnight last night.

Search

File Claws   **Stare**   **Go Hunting**   **So Many Options**   **Window on Birds**

Back to Sleep | Forward To Food | Home Turf | Shred It | Relax | Open One Eye | Open Can | Pounce | Find Toys | Stop & Nap

Location: www.cat-a-list.cat

What's to Eat? | **What's Comfy?** | **Dogless Sites** | **Mouse Search** | **Other Cats** | **Soft Laps**

Cat-a-List
THE SITE FOR INFORMATION

DOWNLOAD NEW SOFTWARE!
CAT-MAP 2000

Shows frequently updated info on the locations of:

- bushes for spraying
- sewers for hiding
- escape holes in fences
- catnip patches
- birds' nests
- puddles and birdbaths for drinking
- ponds with fish
- trees with branches allowing you to climb on roofs
- kind old ladies
- dogs classified by size, speed, and intelligence
- territory of raccoons and possums
- locations of nasty little children

Teasable Dog Lives Here

DOWNLOAD NOW

Waldo, a regular CatFinder Online user and Cat-a-List fan

LIVE CAT-SAT

Click <u>HERE</u> to see photos transmitted from Cat-Sat, the worldwide cat satellite system monitoring the world for mice, and bird and salmon migration.

CATFINDER ONLINE

Enter information about the cat you're looking for, and CatFinder Online will tell you where to look:

Name: **Fluffy the Cat**

Description: **Greyish tabby, white tail**

Hunts: **Birds, occasionally mice**

Favors: **Sunny spots, laundry baskets**

Find That Cat

Back to Sleep
 Forward To Food
Home Turf
 Shred It
 Relax
 Open One Eye
 Open Can
 Pounce
 Find Toys
 Stop & Nap

Location: www.scaredy.cat

| What's to Eat? | What's Comfy? | Dogless Sites | Mouse Search | Other Cats | Soft Laps |

Scaredy Cat

BRINGING YOU THE BEST IN ONLINE CAT HORROR AND MYSTERY

THIS MONTH'S TERRIFYING TALES

- The Tail Twisters, a Ghastly True Account of Blood-curdling Infant Humans
- The Brainwashed Zombie Cats Who Obey Humans and Do Tricks on Command

UNSOLVED CAT MYSTERIES

Shadows: Stalking the Creatures Visible Only to Cats

Sofas: The Mysterious Bermuda Triangle of Toys

Ancient Cat Worship: The Egyptians Had It Right. But What Horrible Catastrophe Ended This Vital Practice?

MOVIE SHOP

Order your favorite scary movies online:
The Washer/Dryer of Doom
Friday the 13th Part 12: Return to The Vet
Frankenstein's Pet
Tales of the Animal Shelter
House of the Squirt Guns
Night of the Living Dogs
The Haunting at Vet House
Microwave of No Return
Planet of the Roaring Vacuum Monsters

Awarded
BEST OF THE NET
by INFO-CAT Search Engine

 AUDIO DOWNLOAD:
Did You Hear That? Identifying Mysterious Sounds Outside the House

File Claws   **Stare**   **Go Hunting**   **So Many Options**   **Window on Birds**

 Back to Sleep   **Forward To Food**   **Home Turf**   **Shred It**   **Relax**   **Open One Eye**   **Open Can**   **Pounce**   **Find Toys**   **Stop & Nap**

Location: www.catatonic.cat

What's to Eat?   **What's Comfy?**   **Dogless Sites**   **Mouse Search**   **Other Cats**   **Soft Laps**

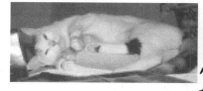 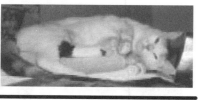

CATATONIC
The Site for Lazy Cats

Welcome to Catatonic, the web site for lazy cats.
We know you need to get back to your nap, so we'll get right to the good stuff.

WHAT'S ONLINE AT CATATONIC?

- **Secret Snoozing Positions of the Burmese**
- **Your Tail: A Mini-Blanket for Your Nose**
- **Humans: Warm Hairless Sofas**
- **Nesting: Clean vs. Dirty Laundry**

DOWNLOAD FREE SOFTWARE
Sun-Tracker 2000

Lets you know where in your house you can catch the best rays at any time of day, or year—even factors in daylight savings time!

Number of Cats Napping Right Now `9998247501`

Number of Cats Napping with One Eye Open `9998247500`

NEW! The Online Nap Guide

Click on a picture to get a full description and how-to for all basic sleeping positions.

File Claws   Stare   **G**o Hunting   So **M**any Options   **W**indow on Birds

Back to Sleep

Forward To Food

Home Turf

Shred It

Relax

Open One Eye

Open Can

Pounce

Find Toys

Stop & Nap

Location: www.basement-land.cat

What's to Eat? | What's Comfy? | Dogless Sites | Mouse Search | Other Cats | Soft Laps

Basement Land
The Indoor Amusement Park for Cats

Water Heaters of the Caribbean

Explore your favorite attraction by clicking on the icon:

ENCHANTED CAN FOREST

Even the littlest kitten will enjoy wondering through the Enchanted Can Forest and looking at the colorful labels depicting peas, corn, and other garden vegetables.

EXTRA SOFA OF

DOOM!

You'll laugh yourself silly at the huge dusty exercise bicycles, flexercisers, abdomenimizers, and pec-o-matics that humans spent good money on, used for a week, and then abandoned. Hours of amusement at the expense of humans.

Human Follywood

As you feel the heat coming off this huge metal cylinder, just close your eyes and you're off to the tropics.

WASHER

There's exciting white water ahead as you ride the rapids of Washer World.

WORLD

What lurks under the old sheet that covers the Extra Sofa of Doom? Springs, spare change, and maybe even abandoned snacks! Best of all, you can claw away at the upholstery to your heart's content and no one will find it for months!

File Claws   **Stare**   **Go Hunting**   **So Many Options**   **Window on Birds**

 Back to Sleep   Forward To Food   Home Turf   Shred It   Relax   Open One Eye   Open Can   Pounce   Find Toys   Stop & Nap

Location: **www.joan_rivercat.cat**

What's to Eat?   **What's Comfy?**   **Dogless Sites**   **Mouse Search**   **Other Cats**   **Soft Laps**

THE *Joan Rivercat* Celebrity Gossip Site
There's No Business Like Meow-Business

Interview

"She Eats Caviar While All She Gives Me Is Kibble and Water!" **Read Joan Rivercat's Exclusive Chat with Horst, Joan Collins's Less-Than-Pampered Pussycat**

Click <u>HERE</u> to sign up for Joan's newsletter: **Gettin' Catty**

Can We Talk?

Chat with glamourous Cindy Clawford and learn her beauty secrets tonight at 9 P.M.

Exclusive

OJ's Cat: "I Ran Away from Home and Moved in with Kato and His Cat."

Back to Sleep | Forward To Food | Home Turf | Shred It | Relax | Open One Eye | Open Can | Pounce | Find Toys | Stop & Nap

Location: www.catnipaholics_anonymous.cat

What's to Eat? | What's Comfy? | Dogless Sites | Mouse Search | Other Cats | Soft Laps

CATNIPAHOLICS ANONYMOUS

ARE YOU A CATNIPAHOLIC? TAKE OUR TEST

1. ☐ Have you ever decided to stop catnip for a week, but lasted only for a couple of minutes?
2. ☐ Do you wish humans and other cats would mind their own business about your catnip and stop telling you what to do?
3. ☐ Have you ever switched from catnip to regular grass or houseplants, in the hope that this would keep you from wanting more catnip?
4. ☐ Have you had to have a bit of 'nip upon awakening from a nap during the past year?
5. ☐ Even though you tell yourself you can quit anytime you want, do you keep finding yourself face down in the catnip patch when you don't mean to?

SUBMIT YOUR ANSWERS HERE

[ENTER]

DON'T LET THIS BE YOU! JOIN CA TODAY!

CA ONLINE MEETINGS

Tonight: Criminalize Catnip?
Tomorrow: Best Rehab Programs for Cats

[CHAT]

CLICK TO CHAT

THE CA 12 PAWSTEPS

1. Step One: Admit you are powerless over catnip.

2. Step Two: Come to believe that a power far greater and bigger than you will probably banish you to the shed outside if you don't give up the evil herb and return to your normal cat self.

Click here to download all 12 pawsteps

HOTLINKS
- **Tuna Anonymous (TA)**
- **Salmon Fanatics International (SFI)**
- **Kittens of Adult Catnipaholics (KAC)**
- **Birdhunters Anonymous (BA)**

File Claws   Stare   Go Hunting   So Many Options   Window on Birds

 Back to Sleep
 Forward To Food
 Home Turf
 Shred It
 Relax
 Open One Eye
 Open Can
 Pounce
 Find Toys
Stop & Nap

Location: **www.sphinx.cat**

What's to Eat? **What's Comfy?** **Dogless Sites** **Mouse Search** **Other Cats** **Soft Laps**

Sphinx The Site for Middle Eastern Cats

Video Download
Watch the Mysterious Dance of the Seven Tails

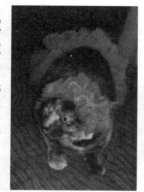

Virtual Reality Tour
Visit the Sahara Desert: World's Largest Cat Box

Recipes
Salmon Hummus Mouse-Kabobs

History on Audio
The Real Story Behind Laurmanx of Arabia, as Read by Omar Shareefeline

Coming Next Week:
Exclusive Interview with Yassir Aracat

73

Back to Sleep
 Forward To Food
Home Turf: IF FOUND CALL:
 Shred It
 Relax
 Open One Eye
 Open Can
 Pounce
 Find Toys
 Stop & Nap

Location: www.ABCat-Sports.cat

What's to Eat?   What's Comfy?   Dogless Sites   Mouse Search   Other Cats   Soft Laps

abCat wide neighborhood of sports

Spanning the neighborhood to bring you the best in cat sports
"The assumption of victory, the disdain of defeat"

Holiday Sports Special

Tune in Saturday, 8 P.M. EST, for Championship Stocking Unstuffing

Program Highlights

Updates on selected sports . . .
- Tinfoil Ball
- Fence Gymnastics
- Shadow Pouncing
- Pointless Racing Around the House
- Championship Faucet Licking

World Champion Faucet Licker, Shadow the Cat

Preview!
Pairs Birdwatching on ABCat

This Week's Females Sports Show Features:
- Cats on Ice
- Skating Cats
- IceCatPades

File Claws   Stare   Go Hunting   So Many Options   Window on Birds

 Back to Sleep
 Forward To Food
 Home Turf
 Shred It
 Relax
 Open One Eye
 Open Can
 Pounce
 Find Toys
 Stop & Nap

Location: www.kittenish.cat

What's to Eat? | What's Comfy? | Dogless Sites | Mouse Search | Other Cats | Soft Laps

Kittenish Fun and Games Online

"Links to the most fun sites on the net for kittens or the kittenish at heart"

GAMEROOM

Play Our Exciting New Interactive Game:
Dog Catcher

Wave at the Human
Click here to activate an electronic paw that will wave at a real human in Pittsburgh.

Play the Classic Mouse-Hunt— Java Version

Go to Siamese.Cat to order your copy of the hilarious new book:
101 Things to Do with a Dead Mouse

CLICK HERE FOR:
Live Toilet Paper Game-Cam

File Claws   Stare   Go Hunting   So Many Options   Window on Birds

 Back to Sleep   Forward To Food   Home Turf   Shred It   Relax   Open One Eye   Open Can   Pounce   Find Toys   Stop & Nap

Location: www.feline-frozen-food.cat

What's to Eat?   What's Comfy?   Dogless Sites   Mouse Search   Other Cats   Soft Laps

FELINE FROZEN FOODS ONLINE—AT-HOME SHOPPING
Frozen Foods Dragged Right to Your Back Door! Just Heat and Eat!

To Order:
Select items, enter your human's credit card information in the box below, then click on "ORDER"

[ORDER]

TODAY'S SALE ITEM: Pigeon Patties, $3.99/lb.

Frozen Bird Selections

Birdfurters, $.99

Birds 'n' Beans, 2/$1

Twitter Tots, $.89

20% OFF Bird Biscuits from the Pussbury Dough Boy

TacoCat Blue Jay Burritos, 3/$5

Cream of Cardinal Soup, 3 cans/$2

Blue Jay Souffle, $3.99

Stow-furs Mockingbird Meatloaf, $3.99

Frozen Mouse Selections

Catsons Mouse Fricassee Frozen Dinners, 3/$5

MouseWatchers Lo-cal Mouse Mousse, $3.99

Cheapo Chicken Fried Mouse, $1.29/lb.

Thrifty Gourmet Dijon Mouse Filets, $2.99/lb.

Meowffer's Mouse Pot Pies, 2 for $3.00

Netscratch

<u>F</u>ile Claws   **Stare**   <u>G</u>o Hunting   So <u>M</u>any Options   <u>W</u>indow on Birds

 Back to Sleep | Forward To Food | Home Turf | Shred It | Relax | Open One Eye | Open Can | Pounce | Find Toys | Stop & Nap

Location: www.aarp.cat

What's to Eat? | What's Comfy? | Dogless Sites | Mouse Search | Other Cats | Soft Laps

---

Sign Up for AARP Now:

Name: [ ]

Nationality: [Calico ▼]
- Persian
- Tabby
- Siamese
- Manx
- Abyssinian

Age: [ ]

[SUBMIT]

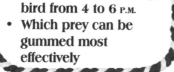

SPECIAL FEATURE:
Dining Out and About

- Early Bird Specials— why it's easiest to bag a bird from 4 to 6 P.M.
- Which prey can be gummed most effectively

AARP

The American Association of Retired Pussycats

Managed Care and Medicat
- Fight Against Drive-Thru Teeth Cleaning for Older Cats. <u>Full story</u>

Antisocial Security
- How to ensure that your humans will take care of you, even if you are old, crotchety, and incontinent. <u>Full story</u>

Today in the Chat Room! GRANDKITTENS
All the cuteness with none of the teat problems

Video Clip

A short excerpt from *Retire to Miami Beach Without Leaving Your House.* This video shows how to re-create the ambience of Miami Beach right in your own home, using only houseplants and your cat box.

GERI-CAT Tabs

Helps you live each of your lives to the fullest!!

Back to Sleep | Forward To Food | Home Turf | Shred It | Relax | Open One Eye | Open Can | Pounce | Find Toys | Stop & Nap

Location: www.cat_tvguide.cat

What's to Eat? | What's Comfy? | Dogless Sites | Mouse Search | Other Cats | Soft Laps

---

TODAY'S BEST BETS

Alleycat McBeel: Alleycat self-deprecatingly bungles yet another heartwarming attempt to mate.

Catista Flockcat as Alleycat McBeel

The Amazing Mouse: Follow the short life of a plump little mouse as it scurries and nibbles, only to meet up with Twinkles, a tabby on a mission, in this Backyard Discovery Channel special feature.

Seinfluff: Episode 36: Hangin' Round the Litter Box: Seinfluff, George, and the nutty next-door cat Kramanx wonder whether they should mate with Elynx. (Rerun)

News and Gossip:
- Foxy TV Network scores hit with *King of the Litter Box.*
- *Regis and Kitty Me* host has catfight with daytime queen, Opurrah.

DAYTIME UPDATE

- *All My Kittens:* Ericat confronts the mysterious scoundrel Coon from Maine with the charge that he has been neutered.
- *Days of Our Nine Lives:* Under the azalea bush, Mr. Paws and Patches square off in a major fight over territory.

Click here for more soap updates:
General Veterinary Hospital
As the Ball Rolls
The Young and the Rex-less

 Audio Downloads

A look back at the five most popular monologues from one of TV's hit sitcoms of the past, *Seinfluff:*
"What is the deal with hairballs, anyway?"
"What is the deal with 'gourmet' cat food, anyway?"
"What is the deal with birds that don't stand still when I'm stalking them, anyway?"
"What is the deal with those automated litter boxes, anyway?"
"What is the deal with leashes for cats, anyway?"

The Inside Scoop on Your Favorite Daytime Dramas:

Things heat up this week as Asa-catt and Dorian get cozy on *Nine Lives to Live.*

Netscratch

File Claws   Stare   Go Hunting   So Many Options   Window on Birds

 Back to Sleep   Forward To Food   Home Turf   Shred It   Relax   Open One Eye   Open Can   Pounce   Find Toys   Stop & Nap

Location: **www.ucatoday.cat**

What's to Eat?   What's Comfy?   Dogless Sites   Mouse Search   Other Cats   Soft Laps

UCA Snapshot

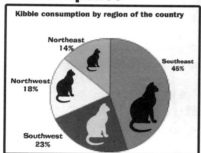

Kibble consumption by region of the country

Northeast 14%
Southeast 45%
Northwest 18%
Southwest 23%

News
Money
Life
Stats

White House Scandal
New Bribery Allegations Regarding Socks the Cat
Caught red-pawed in the act by photographers

George Stephanopolecat and Socks, scheduled for arraignment in bribery scandal later today

Today's Debate

Best way to get humans more money to spend on cats: Vouchers vs. tax breaks

Money

Coalition of Wall Street bankers and investors insist that tax cuts will eliminate the national debt, bring peace to the Middle East, and cure fleas and ringworm

International

Former Communist cats miss regimented schedules of napping

Life

Medical breakthrough: Toe gnawing often removes stickers from paw.

Kittens require milk in early weeks to thrive.

Computers: Computer-aided design creates sofas with maximum shredability.

File Claws   Stare   Go Hunting   So Many Options   Window on Birds

 Back to Sleep   Forward To Food   Home Turf   Shred It   Relax   Open One Eye   Open Can   Pounce   Find Toys   Stop & Nap

Location: www.catsumer-reports.cat

| What's to Eat? | What's Comfy? | Dogless Sites | Mouse Search | Other Cats | Soft Laps |

SPECIAL REPORT
Tail Extenders:
Beauty Aid or
Cheap Ripoff?

Catsumer Reports

Cat Beds: Catsumer Reports rates the mattresses using our exclusive Nap-o-meter.

The Truth About "Natural" Cat Foods

Click to see our latest reports and ratings on . . .

| Cat Toys |
| Cat Pans |
| Cat Foods |
| Cat Collars |
| Brushes |
| Cat Beds |

 Rating Brushes: It Can Save Your Hide!

Toilet Paper Durability and Fun Test Results

HOLIDAY PREVIEW Cat Toys: Are any of them actually remotely interesting?

This Site Has the Good Mousekeeping Seal of Approval

File Claws   Stare   Go Hunting   So Many Options   Window on Birds

| Back to Sleep | Forward To Food | IF FOUND CALL: Home Turf | Shred It | Relax | Open One Eye | Open Can | Pounce | Find Toys | Stop & Nap |

Location: **www.democat.cat**

| What's to Eat? | What's Comfy? | Dogless Sites | Mouse Search | Other Cats | Soft Laps |

⭐DEMOCATIC ⭐NATIONAL ⭐COMMITTEE

 ## International Affairs Special Report

The War in Abyssinia!

DemocatCAM!!

Eye on the White House Litter Box! How to Make YOUR Contribution!

 ## Democatic Position Papers

• **Pro-Choice versus Pro-Life: Are Spaying and Neutering Good for the Population?**

• **Bengayl and Lesbiangora Cats Have Rights, Too**

• **Free Kibble for All Kittens, and Poor, Elderly, Orphaned, and Crippled Cats**

TAKE OUR ONLINE DNC QUIZ!!

How can you tell if you're a Democat or a Republicat? Take our DNC Quiz and find out!

1. Do you approach your food bowl from the left or the right? Click <u>HERE</u> to continue.

 ## Video Clip

Click <u>HERE</u> for a welcome message from the First Cat

SPRAY Our

 **Guest Book!**

 Back to Sleep   Forward To Food   Home Turf   Shred It   Relax   Open One Eye   Open Can   Pounce   Find Toys   Stop & Nap

Location: www.sharper-claw.cat/snack

What's to Eat? **What's Comfy?** **Dogless Sites** **Mouse Search** **Other Cats** **Soft Laps**

THE SHARPER CLAW®
online catalog

Search for

- **Health & More**
- **Home Sweet Home**
- **Great Outdoors**
- **Snack Time**
- **Comfort Zone**

Scratch HERE to order!!

Click HERE to see our "Comfort Zone" Collection for cats who want the Cozy Life!

AquaCat™ Snorkel

Underwater fishing for hours on end has never been easier since the arrival of the Sharper Claw AquaCat™ Snorkel. Fountains, shallow ponds, and streams are no longer hiding places for fishy snacks. Comes with snorkel, mask and mesh basket for storing the catch of the day.

FoodVue™ Kitchen Counter Mirror

You know there might be something good on the kitchen counter, but how can you tell without going to the bother of leaping up there? Just take a glance in the new FoodVue™ Kitchen Counter Mirror and you'll know all. This curved mirror gives a full 180-degree view that lets you find goodies fast! Snacking efficiency at its best!

ArcticAccess™ Refrigerator Cat Switch

Humans are notoriously slow when it comes to opening the refrigerator. Wait no more with our ArcticAccess™ Refrigerator Cat Switch. This secret hidden switch allows instant access to cat food, leftovers—anything in the fridge. And the only downside is irrelevant higher utility bills!

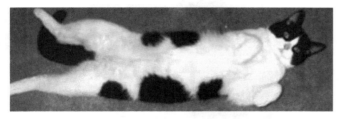

Back to Sleep | Forward To Food | Home Turf | Shred It | Relax | Open One Eye | Open Can | Pounce | Find Toys | Stop & Nap

Location: www.K-Tail.cat

What's to Eat?   What's Comfy?   Dogless Sites   Mouse Search   Other Cats   Soft Laps

K-Tail's Yowlin' in the '60s, '70s, and '80s
A Collection of Your Favorite Pop Hits

Remember the first time you heard the rockin' tunes of that mega-band, Three Cat Night? Or grooved to the smooth moves of the cool cat, Boz Scratch? Well, memories can now be realities, with the best K-Tail collection ever: Yowlin' in the '60s, '70s, and '80s.

Yowlin' in the '60s, '70s, and '80s is a fantabulous collection of your favorite hits of the '60s, '70s, and '80s, and includes hits from some of the most popular bands and recording artists of all time, including:

K-TAIL RECORDS

Get down to the reggae beat of that favorite tune, "I Scratched the Sheriff," and the guitar-rock anthem, "(Eat the) Free Bird." Remember the radical '60s with tunes from Bobcat Dylan, and the piano-driven classic, "Goodbye Yellow Brick Litter Box."

More of your favorite tunes...

"50 Ways to Eat Your Kibble"

"Cat with No Name"

"Honky Cat"

"Cats in the Cradle"

"Born to Be Wild"

The Byrds
Tunaloaf
Cream
Pink Tongue
and more!

More of your favorite artists...
Cat Stevens
Metallicat
The Animals

Hours since "Stairway to the Cat Pan" has played on a Classic Rock radio station **2**

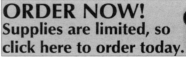

File Claws   Stare   Go Hunting   So Many Options   Window on Birds

Back to Sleep | Forward To Food | Home Turf | Shred It | Relax | Open One Eye | Open Can | Pounce | Find Toys | Stop & Nap

Location: www.republicat.cat

What's to Eat? | What's Comfy? | Dogless Sites | Mouse Search | Other Cats | Soft Laps

Republicat National Committee

Republicat Position Papers

Welfare Reform: Poor Cats Need to Get Off Their Lazy Butts and Stop Lying Around in the Sun

 Do We Need a Strong Defense to Protect Ourselves from the Russian Blues?

State your position!

Eliminate the Food Stamps Program: No More Free Cat Food for the Freeloaders

Spay the Poor and Spare the Rest

E-Mail Mewt
Chief Republicat Member of Congress: Mewt Gingrich

Purrfect Site of the Week Award
FROM
Martha Mewart

We the Cats

Download our Special Report: Because of the Democats, We're Losing the War on Dogs

Click HERE for a Video Message from Our Losing '96 Candidate and Elder Statescat,

Bobcat Dole

Back to Sleep | Forward To Food | Home Turf | Shred It | Relax | Open One Eye | Open Can | Pounce | Find Toys | Stop & Nap

Location: **www.litterati.cat**

What's to Eat? | What's Comfy? | Dogless Sites | Mouse Search | Other Cats | Soft Laps

Essays

Deconstructing Edgar Allan Paw's *Ode to a Food Dish*

T. S. Eliot's Lame Poetic Homage to Cats: A Criticism

Fiction Review

Salmon Yummy's *The Catatonic Verses*

Philosophy

Jean-Paul Catre's *Being, Nothingness, and Kibble*

Litterati

"The Online Litterary Magazine"

SPECIAL REPORT

Ernest Purringway

- *For Whom the Bell on My Collar Tolls*
- *The Old Cat and the Pond*

Theater

Shakespaw's *A Midsummer Night's Prowl*

Number of Pretentious Cats Reading *War and Puss* Right Now:

5 4 2 7 0

New Writers Showcase

My Window, My Life Paean to Myself

<u>F</u>ile Claws   <u>S</u>tare   <u>G</u>o Hunting   So <u>M</u>any Options   <u>W</u>indow on Birds

Back to Sleep

Forward To Food

Home Turf

Shred It

Relax

Open One Eye

Open Can

Pounce

Find Toys

Stop & Nap

Location: **www.career.cat**

What's to Eat? | **What's Comfy?** | **Dogless Sites** | **Mouse Search** | **Other Cats** | **Soft Laps**

Helping Cats Obtain Their Dream Jobs

Career Cat Institute

Not sure what you should do with your life? Is one of your nine lives passing you by? Is everyone else in the fast lane on the success alley except you?

Then you need CCI, the Career Cat Institute. At CCI, we'll help you determine exactly what occupation you're best suited for, and provide the necessary training to put you in a job right away. Just start by taking this simple test. (Click on your preferred options.)

Do you prefer working with your:
A. <u>Paws</u>
B. <u>Mouth</u>
C. <u>Working is a concept beneath me</u>

Would you rather spend time with:
A. <u>Cats who hunt</u>
B. <u>Cats who climb</u>
C. <u>I prefer to be by myself, except for rare moments when I'd like to be petted or complimented</u>

What makes you happiest?
A. <u>Sleeping in the sun</u>
B. <u>Sleeping under the bed</u>
C. <u>Sleeping in whatever location is most pleasing to me at the moment</u>

 CCI Career-Cam

Snowball, our latest career placement success story, hard at work in a satisfying career thanks to CCI's training.

Find Me a Career!

PRELIMINARY RECOMMENDATION:

For your career, we recommend that you . . .

spend most of your time sleeping

File Claws   Stare   Go Hunting   So Many Options   Window on Birds

Back to Sleep   Forward To Food   Home Turf   Shred It   Relax   Open One Eye   Open Can   Pounce   Find Toys   Stop & Nap

Location: www.martha_mewart.cat

| What's to Eat? | What's Comfy? | Dogless Sites | Mouse Search | Other Cats | Soft Laps |

MARTHA MEWART

Shredding

Martha's Crafty Corner

Reverse Macrame: Untie Silly Knots to Reveal Beautiful and Enjoyable Yarn!

The Secret Fun Inside Knitted Sweaters

It's a Good Thing!

Fabulous Low-Cost Avant-Garde Decorating Techniques Using Only Your Claws and a Glue Gun

Curtains That Say "I Was Here"

TAKE OUR ONLINE QUIZ!
How Much Decorating Help Can Your Human Actually Stand Before You're Declawed?

Video Clip

Martha's Latest Project

See Martha Demonstrate How to Perforate Lamp Shades for the Antique Look

File Claws   Stare   Go Hunting   So Many Options   Window on Birds

 Back to Sleep   Forward To Food   Home Turf   Shred It   Relax   Open One Eye   Open Can   Pounce   Find Toys   Stop & Nap

Location: **www.travel-prevention.cat**

| What's to Eat? | What's Comfy? | Dogless Sites | Mouse Search | Other Cats | Soft Laps |

Travel Prevention Online

Frequently Asked Questions:

- What are the seven warning signs of imminent travel?
- How can you stop travel before it even starts?
- How can you bite a human through the bars of your travel carrier and actually draw blood?
- Why is under the gas pedal the comfiest place in a car, and why doesn't your human agree?

Special Report: Road-Trip Tips

- Throwing up for maximum effect
- Flatulence = freedom
- Ten surefire pitiful cries

HIDE-E-HOLE GENERATOR
Enter the name of the airport, or type of airplane, train, bus or highway rest stop to get a list of the best places for a cat to hide.

[Search]

Video Link ◄■

Download highlights from our informational automobile travel video: "Five Obscene Gestures to Make at Dogs Riding in Other Vehicles"

Highlighted FAQ:

- How can you use sumo techniques to stay out of cat carriers?

Last-Ditch Efforts:

Wresting control of the car away from your human

Escape-ometer
Number of Cats That Have Escaped at U.S. Airports and Roadside Rest Stops—Year to Date

9050052006

File Claws   Stare   Go Hunting   So Many Options   Window on Birds

Back to Sleep   Forward To Food   Home Turf   Shred It   Relax   Open One Eye   Open Can   Pounce   Find Toys   Stop & Nap

Location: www.national_curiouscat.cat

What's to Eat? | What's Comfy? | Dogless Sites | Mouse Search | Other Cats | Soft Laps

More Stories:

"Abominable Saber-tooth" Reappears in Pacific Northwest: "Just Its Poop Weighs 400 Pounds!" Say Fearful Park Rangers!

Morris: I Beat Ringworms and Lived!

New Vitamin Guarantees TEN Lives Instead of Nine!!

Litter of Kittens Believed to Be Offspring of Elvis!!!

NATIONAL CURIOUSCAT
America's Favorite Tabbyloid

TODAY'S TOP STORY
Socks and Intern Cat . . .
Discovered Together in Incestuous White House Love Nest

▶▶▶ *GET THE FULL STORY*

<u>CHAT!</u>
Today in the National CuriousCat Chat Room: Talk to Other Cats Who Think They Are Reindeer!

Back to Sleep
 Forward To Food
 Home Turf
 Shred It
 Relax
 Open One Eye
 Open Can
 Pounce
 Find Toys
 Stop & Nap

Location: www.anti-cat-haters.cat

What's to Eat?   What's Comfy?   Dogless Sites   Mouse Search   Other Cats   Soft Laps

THE ANTI-CATHATERS WEB

For Cats Who Hate Humans Who Hate Cats

NEW! Surefire Ways to Spot the Person in the Room Who Hates Cats the Most

FAQs
- How can you be sure they're looking when you spray?
- Where should you leave those little "gifts" so they'll have the most impact?
- How can you increase your shedding around humans who are allergic to cats?

Download
"Turning off the Cat Hater Even More!"
Photos Show You How to Make Sure They NEVER Pick You Up!

Cat HaterCAM
See If You Recognize Today's "Cat Hater of the Day"

Cat Hater-ator
Click on your state, and the Cat Hater-ator will generate a complete list of known cat haters in your area.

File Claws   Stare   Go Hunting   So Many Options   Window on Birds

 Back to Sleep   Forward To Food   Home Turf   Shred It   Relax   Open One Eye   Open Can   Pounce   Find Toys   Stop & Nap

Location: www.fha-hunt.cat

What's to Eat?   What's Comfy?   Dogless Sites   Mouse Search   Other Cats   Soft Laps

WELCOME TO THE FHA

This Site Has the Good Mousekeeping Seal of Approval

THE FELINE HUNTING ASSOCIATION

STALKING TIPS 'N' TRICKS

- Best Places to Find Mice
- Ten New Ways to Catch Your Bird
- Lying Still and Waiting—the Reliable Standby
- Instant Gratification Through Aquariums and Explosives

"Hunting is a right guaranteed in the Catstitution."
—Billy Bob Caterwauler, FHA President

FHA BIRD-O-LATER

Enter your location and preferred bird prey here and receive the bird migration patterns and seasons for YOUR area!

Search

AUDIO CLIP

 Listen to Puss Limbaugh Live

VIDEO CLIP

An excerpt from "Displaying Your Kill," the FHA video that shows you where to put it so your human can't miss it; how to arrange it for maximum impact; and the ultimate display question: headless or not?

Back to Sleep | Forward To Food | Home Turf | Shred It | Relax | Open One Eye | Open Can | Pounce | Find Toys | Stop & Nap

Location: www.calendar-ware.cat

What's to Eat? | What's Comfy? | Dogless Sites | Mouse Search | Other Cats | Soft Laps

Cat Calendar-Ware
Software for the Organized Cat

"Remember that good organization leaves more time for napping."
—Lucy McGillikitty, President and CEO, Cat Calendar-Ware

Download Free Trial Copies of the Following Popular Software Programs:

Spray Scheduler `DOWNLOAD`

Keep track of when to spray each object in your territory for maximum coverage with minimum effort

Furniture Claw Dater `DOWNLOAD`

Lets you track how often you can dig into the furniture without getting tossed out of the house

HumanTracker `DOWNLOAD`

Keeps track of human arrival and departure schedules, as well as when your human is typically available to sit on

StealthyPuss `DOWNLOAD`

Keeps track of when you should hide, such as scheduled visits to the vet or the kennel, or trips in the car

HoliDater `DOWNLOAD`

Lets you know which holidays to ignore (i.e., Labor Day) and which involve gigantic edible birds

Mealtimers `DOWNLOAD`

Tracks the times when:
- You are supposed to get your breakfast
- You are supposed to get your lunch
- You are supposed to get a snack
- You are supposed to get your dinner
- You are supposed to get another snack
- Your humans will be eating
- Other humans will be eating
- Little old ladies in the neighborhood will be cooking

 **Netscratch**

File Claws   Stare   Go Hunting   So Many Options   Window on Birds

 Back to Sleep   Forward To Food   Home Turf   Shred It   Relax   Open One Eye   Open Can   Pounce   Find Toys   Stop & Nap

Location: www.sharper-claw.cat/home

What's to Eat? | What's Comfy? | Dogless Sites | Mouse Search | Other Cats | Soft Laps

THE SHARPER CLAW®
online catalog

Search for

Health & More
Home Sweet Home
Great Outdoors
Snack Time
Comfort Zone

Scratch HERE to order!!

Click HERE to see our "Great Outdoors" Collection for the cat who's back to nature!

The Little Niagara™ Water Dish Tipper

Want to irritate your human by tipping over your water dish again, but simply too tired to do it? No problem. Just call Sharper Claw and wash away your troubles with the Little Niagara™ Water Dish Tipper. Hydraulic pistons work every time on even the largest dish. And, best of all, it's remotely activated so you stay high and dry while the kitchen floods.

Rumblemaster™ Automatic Recorded Purrbox

When you're all relaxed and getting your head rubbed, you don't want anything to get in the way of a nice relaxing nap. But your silly human is likely to stop rubbing if they don't hear purring! Just turn on the Sharper Claw Rumblemaster™ Automatic Recorded Purrbox and your human will hear constant reassuring purring, and keep right on rubbing. Batteries last for up to twelve hours, long enough for most naps.

Double Decker™ Cat Lounger

When there's just not enough space, the Sharper Claw Double-Decker™ Cat Lounger lets two of you lounge in the space of one. The relaxation solution for cramped cats.

Netscratch

File Claws   Stare   Go Hunting   So Many Options   Window on Birds

Back to Sleep | Forward To Food | Home Turf | Shred It | Relax | Open One Eye | Open Can | Pounce | Find Toys | Stop & Nap

Location: www.most-wanted.cat

What's to Eat? | What's Comfy? | Dogless Sites | Mouse Search | Other Cats | Soft Laps

Jon Mathis & Mary J. Shomon
Wanted for:
Revealing Cat Computer Secrets!

AMERICAT'S MOST WANTED

Last Known Whereabouts: Washington, D.C., area

Cats: The slightly prissy calico, Lucy McGillikitty, and scrappy orange tabby, Dave T. Cat.

#205876   #104958

M.O.: Mathis and Shomon allegedly spied on Dave and Lucy while the cats were scratching the 'net. The human pair is accused of having stolen various cat computer secrets and publishing what they've discovered.

Rap Sheet: This is hardly a first literary offense for either human. Mathis has written numerous humorous pieces, including the "inside the Washington Beltway" classic *Pentagon Dining: Or Lunch at the Ground Zero Café.* A few years ago, Shomon did extensive "social" research that led to her Washington-area best-selling humor book, *The Single Woman's Guide to the Available Men of Washington.*

Coincidentally, Shomon met Mathis the night before the *Guide* was released, and after recognizing that he was not one of the men parodied in her book, decided she'd marry him on the spot.

Aliases: Mathis has been spotted currently working as a financial consultant, teacher of nonprofit budgeting, and professional singer. Shomon has also adopted various guises, simultaneously running her own PR firm, working as a web-site designer, and editing several health-related web sites and newsletters.

If you should see these two, immediately contact AMERICAT'S MOST WANTED. And if you see copies of their book, *Scratching the 'Net*, buy them immediately. They must be kept out of the hands of humans at all costs! REPORT A SIGHTING!!!!!!

I have information about Shomon and Mathis!!!

HAVE YOU SEEN THESE FUGITIVES?